SECRETS TO THRIVING IN BABYLON

TIM PASKERT

PUBLISHING

CONTENTS

COPYRIGHT

Author: Tim Paskert

Editor: Eli Gonzalez

Cover Design: Amanda Murray

Published by: The Ghost Publishing, LLC

Paperback ISBN-13: 979-8-9854365-4-9

FOREWORD

Most people will never own a business, run a company, lead an army, hold a powerful political position, or occupy any leadership positions within businesses, armies, or governments. This is true of Christians and non-Christians. This is not an accident. The Bible reveals that God has a long history of selecting those who oppose Him, like Pharaoh, King Nebuchadnezzar, and Nero, to rule over His people. It further reveals God's plan is for "every person to be subject to the governing authorities. For there is no authority except by God's appointment, and the authorities that exist have been instituted by God" (Rom. 13:1 NET).

The fact is that God often chooses those who do not believe in Him to serve in powerful earthly positions. He uses all leaders for His good purposes. The Lord declares, "My purpose will stand and I will do all that I please" (Isa. 46:10b NIV). God has a plan as He selects leaders—some heroes, and some villains—who will play their assigned roles in providing for His people.

This book is for all Christians, those who have not been called to serve as business owners, corporate leaders, generals, priests, pastors, kings, politicians, and those who have. *Secrets to Thriving in Babylon* reveals the Lord's practical ways to serve imperfect leaders in a crazy world. When His ways guide us, we have His peace, love, joy, and purpose as we serve in our proverbial Babylon.

DEDICATION

This book is dedicated to all of us who are serving our Lord through our work in Babylon.

SECRETS TO THRIVING IN BABYLON

1

LIVE IN REALITY

The word Babylon comes from the Hebrew word for confused. We live in a very confusing world. This is not new. The first two chapters of the Bible reveal that God created heaven on earth, but then our ancestors decided they had a better plan, and it's been Babylon ever since.

Sixty-nine percent of the world's population does not believe that Jesus is the Son of God, the promised Messiah, who died on the cross, rose from the dead, and provides peace and eternal life for all who believe (Pew Research, April 5, 2017). Most people in this world are confused about God as they either worship false gods or reject religion and religious considerations altogether.

The numbers reveal, and history confirms, that Christians comprise a minority of the world's population. This does not mean, however, that God has lost control; rather, it affirms that Jesus spoke the truth when He said, "My kingdom is not of this world" (John 18:36a NIV). Jesus was born into a confused world, and He didn't have the majority following Him when He ascended into heaven. If the Son of God didn't get a majority, why should we expect it?

The truth is that, from the beginning, the Lord has always protected a remnant, a minority of the world's population that believes and follows Him through this Babylonian world. The Bible reveals that only a handful of this remnant ever held powerful positions in this world. Most of them were like you and me—people living among and working for those who do not believe.

2

YOU ARE A GOOD FIG

There is not a human being on earth who can control their birth. No one has any power over where they are born or who their birth parents will be. However, the Bible tells us that our Father in heaven knows us before we were placed in our mother's womb and knows these circumstances (Isa. 44:24, Jer. 1:5, Psa. 139:13). So, is a person born into poverty, to bad parents, in a nation that opposes the Lord, loved less by God than one born into a wealthy Christian family in a country that honors the Lord? While we know the proper answer, do we believe it?

Our earthly circumstances have no bearing on our relationship with God. I know of a young man born out of wedlock, into a low-income family, living as a detested minority in a nation that was pagan at best, atheist at worst. This man never received a formal education; he worked hard to learn his stepfather's trade; obeyed the laws of the land, and submitted to the religious and political leaders of the day. He never traveled extensively, never achieved earthly wealth, power, or position, and unfortunately, was murdered by those he was trying to help. I call Him, Jesus the Messiah, the Son of God, my Savior, the Lord. When He rose from the dead, Jesus not only proved that He was the Son of God with the power to save all who call on His name, but also proved that our earthly circumstances are no indication of God's love and favor for His children.

So, why do we often allow our circumstances to steal our joy or to cloud our judgment regarding others who are going through difficult times? Our time on this earth is brief compared to our eternal home in heaven where there are no tears, hunger, disease, or death—just life as God intended when He created the world. When we play each day for eternity, our circumstances lose control over our faith, and God's love, joy, and peace rule our lives.

The Hebrew scriptures recount one of the most significant examples of how circumstances have little to do with God's compassion for His children when the prophet Jeremiah was confused by what he saw happening in Judah. That should make you feel better. If a prophet can be baffled by earthly circumstances, we should not be discouraged when we have our lapses. Like the prophet, when we cry out in our confusion to the Lord, He will answer us, revealing great and unsearchable things we do not know (Jer. 33:3). His answers give us the peace and strength we need to keep going.

Here's the backstory behind Jeremiah's confusion: For hundreds of years, the Lord had been sending prophets to the nation of Judah, warning the leaders and the people to knock it off, to quit claiming to be His children as they worshipped false gods. It had gotten to the point where leaders were encouraging the practice of crazy religious ceremonies that included sexual deviancy and even child sacrifice. While God's patience is unfathomable, the Bible reveals that He comes down hard on those who do evil and try to use His name to justify their actions (Matt. 18:6). Even though most Israelites were rebelling against the Lord, there was a remnant of believers who had never turned from Him. Instead, they continued to worship

Him and did their best to follow the Lord. Jeremiah became very perplexed as he observed their circumstances.

After the Lord had sent His servant, Nebuchadnezzar, the pagan King of Babylon, to conquer Judah, Jeremiah felt great confusion and cried out to the Lord (Jer. 25:9). Did you catch that? The Lord sent a man who did not believe in Him to destroy the nation of Judah, His chosen people. The truth is that, aside from a relatively small remnant of believers, the Israelites had become as corrupt and confused as the enemy nation, so why not send a Babylonian to clean up the mess? Who was better qualified? With the conquering complete, Jeremiah's confusion began.

The Lord knew that, 'A Babylonian's gonna do what a Babylonian's gonna do,' and King Nebuchadnezzar played his role perfectly. After defeating Judah, he systematically selected the best-of-the-best, the brightest and those with the highest character. Even a pagan king knows quality when he sees it. Taking them from their homeland to his own land in Babylon, the king trained them to serve his kingdom, even selecting some to serve on his personal staff. This caused Jeremiah great distress as he realized that Nebuchadnezzar had chosen most of those in God's remnant—those who had never turned away from the Lord—to be taken away from the Holy Land to live in Babylon. The king had left behind the bad leaders, the false teachers, and those who worshipped false gods. The Lord knew that Nebuchadnezzar would take the best for himself and leave the rest behind.

In response to Jeremiah's plea, the Lord gave him a vision of two baskets of figs on the steps of the Temple in Jerusalem. One basket had very good figs, and one basket had very bad figs. Then the Lord explained the meaning, "This is what the Lord, the God of Israel, says: 'Like these good figs, I regard as good the exiles from Judah, whom I sent away from this place to the land of the Babylonians. My eyes will watch over them for their good, and I will bring them back to this land. I will build them up and not tear them down; I will plant them and not uproot them. I will give them a heart to know me, that I am the Lord. They will be my people, and I will be their God, for they will return to me with all their heart'" (Jer. 24:5-7 NIV).

Now there's a plot twist! The Lord revealed to Jeremiah that He was pleased with those He sent away to live in the land of Babylon. He wasn't punishing them; the Lord was rewarding them, promising them that this was for their good and that they would be protected. He would build them up in Babylon, plant them in Babylon, not tear them down, and one day they would return to His Holy Land. The Lord had sent His people into Babylon for their protection.

However, there's another basket... "'But like the bad figs, which are so bad they cannot be eaten,' says the Lord, 'so will I deal with Zedekiah, king of Judah, his officials, and the survivors from Jerusalem, whether they remain in this land or live in Egypt. I will make them abhorrent and an offense to all the kingdoms of the earth, a reproach and a byword, a curse, and an object of ridicule wherever I banish them. I will send the sword, famine, and plague against them until they are destroyed from the land I gave to them and their ancestors'" (Jer. 24:8-10 NIV).

Those people that King Nebuchadnezzar permitted to stay in the Holy Land were not forced to leave their homes, family, and property. In fact, some of these "bad figs" were even left in positions of power. However, the Lord would eventually make them an example to all nations as He would send sword, famine, and plague to destroy them. Make no mistake, the "bad figs" proclaimed the Lord as their God, but their words didn't match what they believed in their hearts, and their actions confirmed their beliefs. In regards to their faith, they were liars. As one of my wise mentors, Bill Spell, liked to say, "You can always be a good example of a bad example."

Think about how excited Jeremiah must have been when he understood that Babylon was part of the Lord's plan for His people, the remnant, who, even though imperfect, loved Him. How smart is God? He uses His enemies to protect His people.

Knowing that the remnant would be living in a culture and subject to a government that did not know Him, the Lord provided instructions for His people to follow. They were commanded not to rebel against the authority He had placed over them, but to prosper in Babylon, build houses, and settle down there, to multiply, and to work to see that Babylon enjoyed peace and prosperity, even praying for the city's prosperity while they continued to seek Him and His ways each day (Jer. 29:1-14). Isn't it interesting that the Lord commanded His people to thrive in Babylon, a chaotic and confused culture, and work for everyone's prosperity? Oh, the genius of God. Peace begets prosperity.

The Bible—and history—reveal that the Lord's Babylonian remnant obeyed His commands and their example stands as the model for His remnant today. "If it is possible, as far as it depends on you, live at peace with everyone," the Apostle Paul encouraged those living under an unfriendly culture and Roman government (Rom. 12:18 NIV). Paul understood that we are witnesses to the kindness and goodness of God, and therefore, we are called to be Christ's ambassadors, peacemakers in our Babylonian world (2 Cor. 5:20). Interestingly, ambassadors can't build the relationships necessary to secure peace without living in the foreign nation they are assigned.

One more word about the basket of bad figs: Our sovereign God knew that they wouldn't obey the commands He had given to His Babylonian exiles. Think about it: If they didn't follow God while ruling themselves, they weren't going to follow Him when pagans were ruling them. Sure enough, history and the Bible reveal that those rotten figs left in the Holy Land plotted and rebelled against their Babylonian rulers, who eventually wiped them out.

If the Lord had left His loyal remnant in the Holy Land, they would have been destroyed when their rotten leadership ignored the Lord's command and rebelled against Nebuchadnezzar. The Lord knows the hearts of all (1 Sam. 16:7). He knew that the fraudulent leaders would rebel, so He sent His children to the only place they would be safe, Babylon itself.

Today, if you are a believer in Jesus Christ, you are one of the good figs. You aren't alone. You are part of a huge basket full of good figs. The Lord has placed you within Babylon to prosper, to multiply, and to seek good for all people. He has called you to be His ambassador, His peacemaker to all who don't know Him. God is not punishing you. Instead, you are being protected as you work to negotiate their peace with God.

Living and serving in Babylon is not a punishment from God; it is an opportunity. Sending Jesus from heaven to earth was not a punishment. He came to offer freedom and salvation for all in a world saturated by Babylonian cultures. Today we have the opportunity to help our family, friends, neighbors— and enemies—in Babylon find the freedom and salvation that only Jesus Christ can provide.

In this world, Babylon is the rule, not the exception. Babylon doesn't know God, the love of God, the wisdom of God, or the commands of God, and therefore, can't experience God's peace. Nevertheless, God established Babylonian authorities and He calls us to obey them. Obeying these authorities is the reality that Christ entered into when He walked on the earth and it's still the world we live in today. When we deny this reality, it leads to self-imposed isolation, cultural irrelevancy, religious legalism disguised as piety, frustration, and missing out on seeing God change the hearts of those who are His enemies.

Our God has not left us without instruction, wisdom, and

power. Rather, He's given us all the authority we need to serve in Babylon. Jesus demonstrated this during His earthly ministry. Admittedly, He did have an advantage because He is the Son of God, but many Christians don't realize that Jesus was modeling what the Hebrew scriptures had already revealed: The ways ordinary people can succeed in thriving in Babylon.

Their lives demonstrate the secrets that still apply today. The only thing that has changed is technology. However, before a Christian can apply these truths, we must first acknowledge the reality of our situation—that we do, indeed, live in Babylon.

3

CHASING THE WIND

Is the person who works at McDonald's rather than Chick-Fil-A of weaker faith? Is their relationship with the Lord strained, or are they less devoted to Him? Is a Christian working diligently for an official in the Chinese government somehow less loyal to the Lord than one who serves as a U.S. senator? Is a Christian who works in the general market media or in Hollywood less focused on Christ than one who works on faith-based films for Christian media? What about a home-schooled Christian versus one that attends public schools? We know the correct answers to these questions in our minds and hearts, but do we live the truth by embracing our roles while accepting that the roles of other Christians in Babylon are of equal importance to our own?

Work has been a part of our lives since our ancestors walked out of Eden. It is a common calling among all people, Christian and non-Christian. This, again, is the genius of God. He utilizes work to create a common ground for all people to interact.

Our jobs are like wealth in that they are neutral. However, it is how we view and use our jobs that makes all the difference. The wealthiest one the world has ever known stated it best, "A person can do nothing better than to eat and drink and find satisfaction in their own toil. This too, I see, is from the hand of God, for without Him, who can eat or find enjoyment? To the person who pleases him, God gives wisdom, knowledge and happiness, but to the sinner He gives the task of gathering and storing up wealth to hand it over to the one who pleases God. This too is meaningless, a chasing after the wind." (Eccles. 2:24-26 NIV). We can enjoy our occupations as a blessing or choose to view them as a curse, but either way, our toil will be used for God's good purpose.

Workplaces are as different as the people who work in them. There are no perfect people; therefore, there are no perfect workplaces. In His wisdom, the Lord plants imperfect people into workplaces to provide for families, help neighbors, and even reveal His kindness to His enemies. The apostle Paul nailed it when addressing Christians working for mean bosses in rough places, "Whatever you are doing, work at it with enthusiasm, as to the Lord and not for people, because you know that you will receive your inheritance from the Lord as the reward. Serve the Lord Christ" (Col. 3:23-24 NET). Here's a simple truth, a Christian's reward is the inheritance we receive from the Lord when we go to heaven.

Another thought about work: In this world, work represents lifeboats. The Lord provides these and asks us to fill them with those perishing in a world that is sinking. Some Christ-followers are given bigger lifeboats (jobs) to save more dying in the icy waters of this world. Your work is the Lord's lifeboat for your family and others. Fill it and thrive. Who wants to arrive in heaven in an empty boat?

How do we fill our lifeboat while we are thriving in Babylon? The answers are both practical and empowered by the Holy Spirit, which will likely surprise many. But, the solutions can be applied anywhere in the world by anyone who calls Christ, Lord.

The Hebrew scriptures in Daniel 1:1-7 tell the story of a Jewish teenager who was part of the remnant that King Nebuchadnezzar took from Judah to serve in Babylon. This teenager was devout in his faith to the Lord. In addition, he was from a good Jewish family and likely enjoyed access to the top echelons of Judah's society. Imagine his horror as he witnessed King Nebuchadnezzar, a pagan Babylonian who did not believe in the God of Israel, destroying his country.

As the story opens, this adolescent, Daniel, was taken from his family, country, and everything familiar. The king, who had destroyed Daniel's life in Judah, selected him to serve his own kingdom. Many scholars believe that serving the king also required Daniel to become a eunuch. And we think we have a rough work environment?

Today, Daniel's situation would be equivalent to Iran conquering the United States and taking a teenager from a wealthy Christian family to Tehran to study at Babylon University to serve the Ayatollah. There are very few Christians in the world who will face a situation as extreme as Daniel's. However, Daniel thrived in Babylon and filled his lifeboat. The timeless lessons learned from Daniel's experience can help any Christian thrive in their own Babylon.

Daniel's new boss was nobody's fool. Nebuchadnezzar was an engineer, an administrator, a general, and a ruler. He even built one of the world's ancient wonders, the Hanging Gardens of Babylon, for his wife. He was a brilliant man who had conquered much of the ancient world with an interesting management style. If you did as instructed and were successful, he'd make you very rich. If you failed in your assignment or disobeyed, he had you killed. You think your boss is tough?

How can a nice Jewish kid from a good home work for such a ruthless man? By remembering who he *really* worked for:

"The earth is the Lord's and everything in it, the world and all who live in it" (Psa. 24:1 NIV). Hundreds of years later, the Apostle Peter would remind Christians living under the Roman Emperor Nero (who would feed many of them to lions), "Show proper respect to everyone, love the brotherhood of believers, fear God, and honor the emperor" (1 Pet. 2:17 NET). Unlike our investment portfolios, God's past performance *is* indicative of His future results. Nero and the Roman Empire are dead. Christ and His church are alive. Interestingly, God used those Roman roads to carry the gospel of Christ all over the world. He continues to use governments and rulers the same way today.

Daniel's confidence in the Lord was not shaped by his circumstances. Therefore, he was able to adjust to his new Babylonian surroundings—which, in reality, were quite nice. He was well housed and fed the same meals as King Nebuchadnezzar. In addition, he and the others were treated very well by the Babylonians. This pagan empire gave them the best education Babylon could provide: culture, traditions, agriculture, astrology, astronomy, religions, law, math, and the difficult Akkadian language.

Their Babylonian overseer also gave Daniel and his friends new names. Daniel's Hebrew name means "God is my judge." His Babylonian name, Belteshazzar, means "Lord, protect the king." Daniel's friend Azariah (in Hebrew, "Yahweh has helped"), was changed to Abednego, which means, "Servant of Nebo" (a Babylonian god). Whether their new names were given to mock them and their God is not important. What is important is that Daniel and his friends knew that their Babylonian names and titles did not define them. They were children of the one true God, and He was the one that had sent them to Babylon. No circumstance could change that fact.

Daniel and his friends lived quite well in Babylon, being provided for in abundance. Sure, there weren't any daily scripture readings, prayer gatherings, familiar religious ceremonies, or even any public acknowledgment of the one true God. However, the Lord watched over them and provided for all their daily needs. This protection and provision were just as the Lord had promised them through the Prophet Jeremiah.

Nonetheless, they lived in a pagan culture under a king who did not honor the Lord. So, did they start planning a rebellion? Did they put together a five-year plan to impact their community for Yahweh to change the culture? And finally, did they seek to escape to a more "Yahweh-friendly" land? While there is a time for every season, to pursue any of these three options would have been like chasing the wind.

The Lord had called them to live, settle down, build, pray, work for peace, and thrive in Babylon. He has called Christians to do the same today (John 17:18). Some Christians will labor in ministries or faith-based businesses; others will work in companies filled with those who do not know the Lord. Still, all labor in some way is accomplished in Babylon. Occupations, titles (or lack of titles), and bank accounts do not define Christians. God defines us, and He calls us His children, heirs to His kingdom, which is not of this world. Nothing can change what He has ordained.

Keep in mind that God does not force people to believe in Him. He does not force people to worship Him or to follow Him. Babylon forces people to do things, but God doesn't. So let us not chase the wind by demanding that employers and authorities who don't believe in Christ form a Christian-friendly culture. This is not the example Christ revealed when He walked on this earth.

Like Daniel, may our faith and obedience to the Lord and the earthly authority He has placed us under not be undermined by Babylon's opinions or ideas. Instead, may we enjoy the provision of Babylon, take no offense at their errors, forgive their mistakes as Christ forgives ours, and build the relationships necessary for someone to trust climbing into the lifeboat Christ has provided. We can avoid living in the frustration of chasing the wind if we do these. Instead, we can find fulfillment as we float in our God-ordained Babylonian lifeboats filled with family, friends, and former enemies. Once inside the boat, we can raise the sail to catch the wind of God's peace and provision as we ride through a chaotic world.

4
_____

WHAT IF YOUR EMPLOYER OFFENDS YOU?

The spirit of offense runs rampant in Babylon. This spirit, like a virus, infects its victims with anger, frustration, jealousy, pride, envy, deceit, and hostility. It is contrary to the Holy Spirit, who provides love, joy, peace, patience, goodness, kindness, gentleness, faithfulness, and self-control (Gal. 5:22-23). The truth is that someone will do or say something offensive to God and His children wherever we go.

Giving in to the spirit of offense contaminates businesses, families, friends, churches, and Bible studies. Christians, therefore, should be the least offended and offensive people in Babylon because the anti-virus has been given to us: The Spirit of God, who empowers us to overcome.

Don't worry. I'm not going on a theological tangent regarding the power we have to overcome. There's nothing wrong with that tangent—it's a powerful truth. Instead, I want to emphasize practical ways to deal with the spirit of offense, and the Book of Daniel provides great lessons.

The Hebrew scriptures reveal that while Daniel and his friends were given the best Babylon could provide, it didn't take long for the Babylonians to do something very offensive. The foods and wines provided to Daniel were the same as the king's. This was no prison gruel, only the best available was provided. Nevertheless, King Nebuchadnezzar's food was obtained primarily through ceremonial sacrifices to his pagan gods. The Lord had decreed that His children were not to participate in pagan religious sacrifices (Ex. 20:3, 2 Ki. 22:17). Generational disobedience to this command had ultimately caused the Lord to allow Judah to fall, so Daniel knew that he didn't want to get on that ride again.

The teenager, Daniel, finds himself in a predicament. The authorities are providing their best foods and expecting him to accept their kindness. To refuse their hospitality would be highly offensive to his host, and dangerous. What should he do? Obey God or the authorities? The simple Sunday School answer is to obey God. Obedience to Him is a given. The problem is that we are correctly answering the wrong question. When the leaders we serve give an order that contradicts God's commands, the correct question is, "Lord, how do you want me to handle this?" By asking the Lord the right initial question, it eliminates a lot of needless drama and fretting.

Based upon Daniel's reaction, the Hebrew scriptures reveal that seeking the Lord's solution was his primary focus and it was not infected by the spirit of offense. Think about it. How could Daniel expect people who did not know God to obey His commandments? Because of the Lord's patience and compassion for those who do not know Him, He is not easily offended. God's got thick skin. We need to follow Daniel's example who was determined to obey God and not participate in Babylon's pagan dining (Dan. 1:7). There was a proper way to go about this though. And, Daniel's actions revealed several secrets to dealing with the offense of Babylon.

First, Daniel went to the man he thought was in charge, the overseer of the court officials, and privately asked permission not to participate in the Babylonian meal plan (Dan. 1:8). Please notice that he did not demand to be excused based upon his religious beliefs. There is no indication that Daniel even mentioned God to the overseer. Daniel wasn't seeking conflict; he wasn't trying to stir up the other Jews or embarrass the Babylonians.

Secret to Thriving in Babylon: Daniel sought a private meeting and asked permission to not participate.

Rather than demanding our way or the highway, we should seek to resolve problems privately with authorities. *Never put the king in a position to prove he is the king.* Instead, respectfully make requests and keep the encounters confidential.

Daniel did his part by submitting his request humbly to the overseer. The scriptures reveal that God honored Daniel's obedience by giving him favor with the overseer. Still, the overseer didn't grant Daniel's request. He gave Daniel something much more critical—information. The overseer became transparent with Daniel, revealing that he was too frightened of his boss, King Nebuchadnezzar, to change the meal plan. Daniel and his buddies were prized recruits. If they became weak or sick and the king discovered that they weren't eating the foods he had required, the overseer would be a dead man (Dan. 1:9-10).

Daniel had followed the Lord's ways in handling the offense, but he didn't get what he wanted—a new diet. Instead, he got what he needed—knowledge of the landscape of his new environment. The overseer had a great job title and the appearance of power, but a terrifying boss micromanaged him. He was not empowered to make decisions and could only report what was happening to a boss he feared. Imagine the overseer's daily dilemma as he tried to live in that environment without the Lord's guidance and strength. The man was more of a prisoner than Daniel.

The overseer's situation is not dissimilar to most of the people we report to today in our jobs. Despite their titles, these leaders are ordered to implement plans they did not design, have no authority to adjust, and are held accountable for goals they did not set. Failure to achieve these goals results in their termination rather than extermination, as in Daniel's day. *Therefore, the employee that is sensitive to their boss's plight can be a powerful witness for Christ.*

The overseer denied Daniel's request, but Daniel had discovered that this individual was running scared. Daniel had a choice to make. Should he go over the overseer's head to the king? Should he disobey the overseer and change his diet anyway? Or, should he organize a hunger strike for the God of Israel, which would likely get the man who refused his God-honoring request killed? Well, that would show those Babylonians not to mess with him and his God! Should he drop his appeal and go along with the meal plan? The answer was none of the above. He sought the One above.

Daniel's subsequent actions reveal the practical wisdom of God, who desires unbelievers to turn to Him, be saved, and live eternally with Him. Daniel didn't go over the overseer's head; he went under his nose. He went to the person who reported to the overseer, the warden directly responsible for his care and that of his friends. The proposal was simple. The current meal plan was very generous, but they were eating foods that weren't agreeing with their digestive systems, which were accustomed to much simpler foods. Daniel proposed a limited ten-day test to reveal whether a return to their native diet made them healthier (Dan. 1:11-14).

The boy was now speaking the language of Babylon. A low-profile test, with just four people, yielding a quantifiable result over a short period—low risk, high reward. Even thousands of years ago, no one got into trouble testing a theory, particularly within Babylon, a culture that cherished knowledge. After all, everyone agrees that testing theories is a key to learning.

So what happened? *Daniel sought to honor God rather than elevate himself or destroy those against him,* God took it from there. The warden conducted the test, it was successful, and from that point on, Daniel and his friends were no longer required to eat food the Babylonians had sacrificed to idols. Plus, God endowed these four with knowledge and skill that enabled them to master all sorts of Babylonian literature and wisdom.

God even gave a special gift to Daniel that would allow him to interpret dreams (Dan. 1:15-20). This was all accomplished without placing the overseer in danger. Years later, the overseer would present Daniel and three of his friends to King Nebuchadnezzar as the top of the class of "Babylon U." All of them would serve the king for many years (Dan. 1:15-20).

Several decades ago, I worked at a huge, general market television station. My boss, a man who loved to entertain, spent months organizing a large "Season Premier" client party, overlooking no detail. One of the biggest surprises at the party was to be a "flash mob" dance performed by all station employees. So that everyone would be prepared, my employer arranged extensive rehearsals. There's nothing wrong with that. The dance, unfortunately, celebrated the acceptance of a specific sin, and all sin is detestable to the Lord.

After praying, I went to see my boss privately and asked for permission not to participate in the dance. He asked, "Why?"

"It's personal. Besides, I have no rhythm," I responded.

Some might say, "Why did you not ask for the dance to be canceled?"

The boss planned the party and never asked for my opinion. Why should I offer it unsolicited?

Others might say, "Why did you not point out that the dance and song were offensive to the Lord?"

God doesn't need me to defend Him.

After a brief silence, my boss approved the request. I thanked him and assured him that I would work hard to make his event a success. On the night of the party, I was the first to arrive, the last to leave. I did my very best to ensure every guest enjoyed the experience. My boss noticed this, and until the day he retired, he quietly supported my ministry efforts, which required me to be away from work for a few business hours each week. This favor enabled me to minister to people for many years, and God used a general market television station to pay my bills. Like Daniel, I did my part and let God do His.

Daniel's example still serves as the model of how we are to deal with the offenses of Babylon. Christians should be the most unoffended people in the world. Cultures don't define God, and they don't define us. There is no indication that the king or the rest of Babylon adopted Daniel's diet plan. Why? Daniel's diet was a sincere act of worship on his part. Sincerity is an individual act, not a cultural one.

Throughout Daniel's life, he was never distracted, surprised by, or offended by the culture of Babylon. Changing the culture was never his focus. Instead, honoring God by doing his best to serve the authorities he was placed under is the message of Daniel's life. His model of loving obedience to the Lord still changes hearts today and saves lives for eternity.

Cultures come and go, but eternal life is everlasting. A focus on serving God in Babylon rather than changing, correcting, or fleeing Babylon will result in a life that experiences God's peace amongst chaos.

5

HOW TO GET PROMOTED IN BABYLON

Employers know that high-quality employees are essential for success. When seeking an electrician, is Babylon looking for someone who can quote John 3:16 but thinks AC/DC is an evil 70's rock band? Or, is an educated and highly-skilled electrician who can make sure the lights work without burning down the house preferred? Should a plumber who has no training be hired from a Bible study or someone who has been specifically instructed in the trade? Babylon doesn't care what god you worship; it just wants its plumbing to work.

Employers are similar to college football coaches. If a coach recruits slow, lazy players, winning will be difficult. So instead, the best coaches recruit the best athletes who can play specific positions. Success depends on each athlete working hard, learning continually, and playing the assigned role. No matter how talented a recruit or great the coach, they will fail if they do not work hard and continue to learn. Individual failure impacts the entire team.

As declared in chapter three, we Christians should be striving in our jobs as if working for the Lord (Col. 3:23). We aren't called to be perfect, but our effort should always be excellent. For example, if we are salespeople, we should know our product better than anyone and never become weary of telling prospects about its benefits. Many in administration, accounting, maintenance, production, and marketing depend upon a salesperson's efforts to generate revenues that produce the salaries that feed their families.

What about those who work in building maintenance? Watch how quickly productivity and revenues fall when equipment or the plumbing don't work correctly. Whatever our trade or role in a company, we should practice it with excellence, striving to be the most educated in our position and the hardest working.

Education has always been critical to thriving in Babylon because education was cherished even in ancient times. Today, we are the most educated generation in the history of the world. Access to information is abundant. Modern-day Babylon is full of schools. There are public schools, private schools, religious schools, technical schools, trade schools, charter schools, sports academies, virtual schools, and home schools, and that's before we even start talking about colleges. Breaking news: After we complete our formal education and enter the working class, our education begins in earnest. The truth is, wise people are always learning.

Today, only a handful of people are blessed with the opportunity to attend academically excellent parochial schools or be home-schooled. Thus, most of the world's Christians will not receive an education based on Biblical values. Are these Christians cursed or forsaken by God? Is God punishing them by not allowing them to attend a school that honors Christ? Of course not. Indeed, Moses played a pretty prominent role in God's plan, and the Egyptians educated him. Ol' Moses turned out all right.

Education is like a hammer that can either build or

damage. Furthermore, how a worker uses their education tool determines the success of the assigned task. Learning should create a Christian's value in Babylon, not destroy their faith. We don't go to school to learn about God; instead, we live for Him while attending our classes.

Daniel, Shadrach, Meshach, and Abednego exemplify what to do with a Babylonian education. The Hebrew scriptures tell us they were taken from their comfortable lives in Judah and forced into the conquering king's service. They did not experience school choice in Babylon and were told what they would study. There was no morning prayer or chapel to start the school day, and there were no Bible clubs. They enjoyed none of the wonderful faith-based policies practiced by parochial schools today. Yet, despite these seeming disadvantages, Daniel, Shadrach, Meshach, and Abednego's faith in the Lord flourished while they were at "Babylon U".

Daniel and his friends excelled in their Babylonian education and finished at the top of their class (Dan. 1:18-20). This means that they learned math, science, engineering, astronomy, agriculture, and the tough Akkadian language. In addition, Babylonian astrology and pagan religions, abhorrent to the Lord, were also taught. Nonetheless, their class ranking and strong faith in the Lord demonstrate that they were not required to accept these as truth while learning them.

There is a difference between being asked the name of the Babylonian sun god on a test and *believing* in the sun god. Daniel and his mates understood this as they studied, learned, and graduated. Excelling in their studies brought them to the king's attention. Nebuchadnezzar discovered that they were far better than all the Babylonian magicians and enchanters who practiced Babylon's false religions. The king then promoted these four young Jewish men to serve in the most powerful empire in the world.

Their Babylonian education reveals four secrets that can be applied by Christians today:

1. Where we are educated should not negatively impact our faith. Our God is a lot bigger than any school.
2. Education is the currency of Babylon.
3. Strive to become the most educated in whatever profession we pursue.
4. Education is a cornerstone to successfully thriving in Babylon.

The more educated in providing a product or service needed by people, the more valuable and likely for promotion in Babylon. Excel in becoming an expert in the profession the Lord has called us to serve within. Always strive to learn more, and we will find ourselves thriving within the chaos of life in Babylon while enjoying a solid relationship with Christ.

6

WHAT IF YOUR BOSS MAKES A STUPID DECISION?

D o you ever make mistakes? We all do. Then why do we expect our bosses to be perfect? They make mistakes just like us. The name of this chapter is a mistake. Alternatively, "What to do *When* Your Boss Makes a Stupid Decision?" is a better title.

Whether they are Christians or not, leaders can make terrible decisions that cause great suffering. The authorities of this world are fallible, but that doesn't change a Christian's call to submit to the power the Lord has placed over us. God's peace comes to Christians in the workplace when we quit expecting our bosses to be perfect.

Instead, we are to seek God's wisdom to help our bosses overcome their errors.

Again, we can look at Daniel, and his buddies, Shadrach, Meshach, and Abednego. As previously discussed, they were part of the exiled remnant who loved the Lord and had not turned from His ways. Yet, they served a ruthless empire led by an unbelieving king who had conquered their land and families.

History reveals that King Nebuchadnezzar was a brilliant

leader, general, administrator, civic planner, engineer, and architect. During his life, the king was the most powerful man in the world. His word was the law of the land. However, the second chapter of Daniel reveals that despite his great successes, the king was stressed. He had dreams every night that he didn't understand. It was tormenting him, almost to the point of insanity.

"So the king summoned the magicians, enchanters, sorcerers, and astrologers to tell him what he had dreamed. When they came in and stood before the king, he said to them, 'I have had a dream that troubles me, and I want to know what it means'" (Dan. 2:2-3 NIV).

The king does not know God or His ways, so he does what he thinks is right. He summons his most trusted advisors. It's amazing that such an intelligent man would have placed so much trust in a group of liars and frauds. Even a small child who loves God could have avoided choosing these frauds as advisors. Since Moses' time, God had warned believers to have nothing to do with magicians, enchanters, sorcerers, or astrologers (Deut. 18:9-14). These advisors were frauds. But King Nebuchadnezzar doesn't know the Lord or His statutes and decrees. He is desperate, sleep-deprived, distraught, and he did the only thing he knew to do.

Secret to Thriving in Babylon: Realize that the authorities we serve can be anxious over issues we can't see.

Think about it. Leaders and authorities are people, just like us. They have all sorts of personal, family, and health problems, just like us. Plus, they have to deal with the messes other people create. How would you like to be the person deciding how to deal with a terrorist regime while also handling family issues and political enemies who constantly seek to undermine your governing authority? How would you sleep knowing that your next decision could impact the entire planet?

As followers of Jesus the Messiah, we are called to obey the earthly authorities God has placed us under and pray for them, remembering that they, too, are dealing with issues. Everyone who believes in Christ becomes an advisor to the authorities we serve when we pray for them. We may never meet all of those placed over us, but we can rest in knowing that the Lord will handle them, the easy way or the hard way.

The fraudulent advisors answered the king, "May the king live forever! Tell your servants the dream, and we will interpret it" (Dan. 2:4 NIV). Yep, flattery, brown-nosing, and redirecting a straightforward command are not new techniques for the deceivers of this world. But the king was nobody's fool as he replied to his advisors, "This is what I have firmly decided: If you do not tell me what my dream was and interpret it, I will have you cut into pieces and your houses turned into piles of rubble. But if you tell me the dream and explain it, you will receive from me gifts and rewards and great honor. So tell me the dream and interpret it for me" (Dan. 2:5-6 NIV).

Even though the king knew his advisors' character and was aware of their manipulative ways, he continued to seek their counsel. He was accustomed to dealing with them and revealed his management style—the 'carrot and whip' incentive plan. Greed and fear are still powerful incentives used in Babylonian culture. Give me what I ask, and I will make you wealthy. Fail, and you will suffer. Nebuchadnezzar set clear-cut goals: Tell me my dream and interpret it. He then eliminated any opportunity to cheat the system by not providing additional information. Instead, the king laid out a well-defined problem, the goals, the compensation, and the consequences of failure on an equal playing field. All had the same opportunity. The king wanted answers and didn't care who had them, but insisted that they be correct answers.

Nebuchadnezzar wasn't concerned with reporting to Human Resources. He *was* Human Resources, though defined a little different than today. In other words, if you were human, you were his resource. Outside of a handful of countries, most Christians live within systems where the authorities they report to answer to no one in this world. Even in countries with laws that protect employees, the management system of greed and fear is standard. The consequences of failure are not losing your life, as in Daniel's day, but your livelihood.

The greed/fear-based management system was, is, and always will be stressful to all, regardless of faith. Though the advisors knew the king's power over them, they did what Babylon does. They badgered the king to give them what they wanted, the dream, and when he wisely refused, they complained publicly, "There is no one on earth who can do what the king asks! No king, however great and mighty, has ever asked such a thing of any magician or enchanter or astrologer. What the king asks is too difficult. No one can reveal it to the king except the gods, and they do not live among humans" (Dan. 2:10-11 NIV).

The advisors' response is Babylonian in nature. They are publicly arguing with the one in authority, "We have rights. This isn't fair. You can't do this to us! Do you know who we are? You're nuts! What you are asking can't be done!" The problem is that their response was Biblically incorrect. God's truth applies to all people, regardless of their faith, and He says, "...a harsh word spurs anger," and "the wrath of a king is like a messenger of death" (Prov. 15:1b NIV; Prov. 16:14a NET). Southern translation, "When you mess with the bull, you get the horns." Their answer wasn't respectful or wise, forcing the king to prove his authority.

Without offering to find a solution, they pushed back hard

against the command of a powerful, weary, and tormented king. This pushback from the magicians and astrologers gave Nebuchadnezzar a simple choice: Break his word regarding the consequences of failure and lose face, or follow through. It wasn't a difficult decision. "This made the king so angry and furious that he ordered the execution of all the wise men of Babylon. So the decree was issued to put the wise men to death, and men were sent to look for Daniel and his friends to put them to death" (Dan. 2:12-13 NIV).

The consequences of the advisors' decision brought down wrath on many people who weren't even at the meeting. Even though they had nothing to do with the advisors' foolish response to the king, Daniel and his three friends were in grave danger.

Failure to obey authority can result in unexpected consequences upon the innocent. Obedience to God's word may not prevent the collateral damage of a king's wrath, but it stops being the *cause* of the wrath. If we aren't the cause, then we're part of the solution. We are part of God's disaster response team by saving others from the devastation of wrath. We are not victims of other people's poor decisions; rather, we are first responders and rescuers.

At this point, it's essential to note that King Nebuchadnezzar had not asked his advisors to break any laws of the land or any of God's commandments. Instead, a dream was tormenting the man. He was desperate. In his Babylonian way, he was crying out for help.

Secret to Thriving in Babylon: Bring God's perspective to every problem. Are you being asked to do something wrong in God's sight, or is the task just difficult to accomplish?

God's children are not to respond as Babylonians, but as God directs. "A gentle answer turns away wrath, but a harsh word spurs anger. The tongue of the wise adorns knowledge, but the fool gushes folly" (Prov. 15:1-2 NIV). Daniel would be used to demonstrate the wisdom of God's truth. "The wrath of a king is like a messenger of death ... but a wise person appeases it" (Prov. 16:14 NET).

Daniel and the three amigos were not at the king's meeting for some unknown reason. Can you imagine Daniel's surprise when the king's guards showed up at the 'ol' hacienda'? "When Arioch, the commander of the king's guard, had gone out to put to death the wise men of Babylon, Daniel spoke to him with wisdom and tact. He asked the king's officer, 'Why did the king issue such a harsh decree?' Arioch then explained the matter to Daniel. At this, Daniel went to the king and asked for time, so that he might interpret the dream for him" (Dan. 2:14-16 NIV).

Daniel had received the king's messenger of death with wisdom and tact. He didn't demand his rights, "He can't do this to me! Call my attorney! I'll sue! We're talking class action! Wait 'til the cable networks hear about this. The headlines will be, 'The King Bullies Innocent Jewish Immigrant.'"

Nope, he didn't respond in a Babylonian way, but rather as a child of God. Daniel asked a simple question, "Why would the king issue such a harsh order?" He tactfully did not question the king's authority to issue the command; instead, he politely asked the reason for it.

Daniel's godly reaction to the reason for such a harsh edict opened the door for a miracle that would save many lives. Unlike the other Babylonian wise men, he went directly to the king, stated that he understood the assignment, and asked for time to complete the work. In doing so, he appeased the king's wrath.

Daniel did not know the answer. He just respectfully asked for time to work on it. This was the same problem that the magicians and enchanters faced, but Daniel had a different reaction to it. Our tone and words when addressing authority impact others, including our families. React biblically, not *Babylonially*.

Nebuchadnezzar granted Daniel's request the following morning, albeit with a tight turnaround. So, maybe that's where the term deadline originated? "In the morning, or ya'll will be dead-in-a-line."

The example revealed in this story is still the model for Christians today. Without complaint, Daniel went home, told his three friends the king's assignment, and then took the problem to the only One who could provide them with the answer—God. They prayed.

I know what you're thinking, *When in a tough spot, pray. Thanks for the tip, Captain Obvious!*. However...

Secret to Thriving in Babylon: Know how to pray when in a tight spot.

That is what Daniel's story reveals. He and his friends didn't ask God to strike down the king; they didn't complain to the Lord about the king; they didn't blame God for putting them in this impossible situation. They also didn't pray for a political cue. They simply asked the Lord for mercy and to provide the answer to the king's problem.

Since the Bible tells believers to do this kind of praying, no one should be surprised by what happened next. God answered them that night. Why so quickly? The Lord's timing is always perfect. If they hadn't received the answer that night, death would have come in the morning. Our heavenly Father always knows the correct time and is always punctual.

In the Bible, our Holy Father in heaven gives His children a 'double-dog-dare,' "I, the Lord, do these things. I, the Lord, form the plan to bring them about. I am known as the Lord. I say to you, 'Call on me in prayer and I will answer you. I will show you great and mysterious things that you still do not know about' (Jer. 33:2-3 NET). Four desperate men took the dare, asked, and received. Now came the tricky part. Would they believe what they had received, or would they doubt?

Ever since God created humanity, doubting has been the challenge. Will we believe God when He answers us? Will we take Him at His word (the scriptures) and act, or will we doubt His answers and the scriptures? This pattern started in Eden and continues today, "'Did God really say that you must not eat from any tree in the garden?'" (Gen. 3:1 NIV). Jesus' half-brother, James, clarified God's 'double-dog-dare' perfectly, "If any of you lacks wisdom, you should ask God, who gives generously to all without finding fault, and it will be given to you. But when you ask, you must believe and not doubt, because the one who doubts is like a wave of the sea, blown and tossed by the wind. That person should not expect to receive anything from the Lord. Such a person is double-minded and unstable in all they do" (James 1:5-8 NIV).

Ask God for wisdom, and He will answer. It's a promise.

Secret to Thriving in Babylon: Ask for wisdom, then receive, believe, and act on the wisdom.

It will not always be easy, but you will find peace in your follow-through. When God gives us wisdom and then we doubt, we are like the ancient Babylonian advisors: without direction, rudderless, and at the mercy of an angry king rather than a loving God.

The question isn't whether God will answer, but what we

will do with the answer He provides. Daniel shows us how to respond, "Let the name of God be praised forever and ever, for wisdom and power belong to him. He changes times and seasons, deposing some kings and establishing others. He gives wisdom to the wise; he imparts knowledge to those with understanding; he reveals deep and hidden things. He knows what is in the darkness, and light resides with him. O God of my fathers, I acknowledge and glorify you, for you have bestowed wisdom and power on me. Now you have enabled me to understand what we requested from you. For you have enabled us to understand the king's dilemma" (Dan. 2:20 - 23 NET).

Daniel praises and thanks God with the enthusiasm of a child receiving a surprise sundae on a hot summer day. He's grateful and acknowledges God's complete authority, wisdom, and knowledge of things unknown to humankind, and Daniel commits to using the understanding for God's glory. The Lord's wisdom provides light in the caves of this world to guide those who use it to flick the switch.

This prayer leaves little doubt that Daniel intends to act on the knowledge he has gained. It's essential to note that the Lord only provides what we need to know to take our next step of faith. God provided Daniel with the wisdom he needed to answer the king's question. But, He did not tell Daniel how the king would react.

"Then Daniel went to Arioch, whom the king had appointed to execute the wise men of Babylon, and said to him, 'Do not execute the wise men of Babylon. Take me to the king, and I will interpret his dream for him'" (Dan. 2:24 NIV).

Daniel is a man of faith and action. Arioch is preparing for the executions when one of the dead-men-walking says, "Hold it! Drop the ax and back away. I've got the answer the king seeks." Daniel's request reflects God's character, "Do not execute the men of Babylon." The Lord extends his mercy to all people. These "wise" men did not believe in the one true God.

But, their unbelief did not stop God from offering His mercy, "As surely as I live, declares the Sovereign Lord, I take no pleasure in the death of the wicked, but rather that they turn from their ways and live. Turn! Turn from your evil ways! Why will you die ... ?" (Ezek. 33:11 NIV).

Secret to Thriving in Babylon: Remember, God's wisdom is offered to all people; it is never to be used by anyone for self-promotion.

Realize that some will receive this understanding and knowledge, find the Lord, and be saved, while others will reject it. Our job is to be faithful in providing the Lord's insight to all, not just the bosses and co-workers we like. God wants *all* people to benefit from His wisdom.

So, over 2,500 years ago, a young Jewish exile student from 'Babylon U' found himself standing before an angry, tired, tormented king who also happened to be the most powerful man in the world. Life and death hung in the balance. David versus Goliath—round two. Except Daniel didn't even have a slingshot. To those observing, Daniel appeared to be an underdog standing defenseless against a mighty king. But Daniel wasn't the underdog. The Lord, the Maker of heaven and earth, was with him. And just like Goliath, King Nebuchadnezzar never had a chance!

Humbly—*humbly!*—Daniel revealed both the king's dream and the interpretation. He did not lecture, preach, or go beyond the assignment. Instead, he provided the requested information and concluded his report by saying, "The great God has shown the king what will take place in the future. The dream is true and its interpretation is trustworthy" (Dan. 2:45b NIV). Then he waited in silence to see how the most powerful man in the world would react to God's revealed truth.

"Then King Nebuchadnezzar fell prostrate before Daniel and paid him honor and ordered that an offering and incense be presented to him. The king said to Daniel, 'Surely your God is the God of gods and the Lord of kings and a revealer of mysteries, for you were able to reveal this mystery'" (Dan. 2:46-47 NET).

The most powerful man in this world is no match for the great "I AM." Nebuchadnezzar fell flat on his face at the feet of an enslaved Jewish immigrant with an appointment for Arioch to chop-cut at noon. The king's response indicated that his heart was for the truth. He didn't care where the truth came from, he just wanted the truth. He was an honest skeptic. He cared more about knowing the truth than he did about being right.

Secret to Thriving in Babylon: Never underestimate the power of God's wisdom when received by an honest skeptic.

The humbled king acknowledged Daniel's God as "the God of gods." Nebuchadnezzar isn't turning away from his false gods yet, but this marks the beginning of his journey to faith in the one true God, the God of Abraham, Isaac, and Jacob. Through the interpretation of his dream, the Lord had given the king peace in place of despair and vengeance.

"Then the king elevated Daniel to high position and bestowed on him many marvelous gifts. He granted him authority over the entire province of Babylon and made him the main prefect over all the wise men of Babylon" (Dan. 2:48 NET).

Nebuchadnezzar's actions demonstrated a powerful truth. "In the Lord's hand the king's heart is a stream of water that he channels toward all who please him" (Prov. 21:1 NIV). Daniel had pleased the Lord by praying, receiving, believing, and acting. Daniel met the king's need, and now the Lord maximized the generational impact of this simple act by moving the king to promote Daniel to a powerful position within Babylon. Daniel would now be the boss of the men he had saved, the king's Babylonian wise men.

Daniel's reaction to the promotion reveals something significant. "And at Daniel's request, the king appointed Shadrach, Meshach, and Abednego over the administration of the province of Babylon. Daniel himself served in the king's court" (Dan. 2:29 NIV). Daniel realized that no man is an island. The Bible says, "Though one may be overpowered, two can defend themselves. A cord of three strands is not quickly broken" (Eccles. 4:12 NIV). He remembered his loyal friends who were very competent and dedicated to the Lord.

Before closing this story, there's one more big secret that's often overlooked. Who did God use to promote Daniel and his three amigos? King Nebuchadnezzar was the man who had conquered their homes and their nation. The one who had brought death and destruction down on Daniel and his friends' families and fellow citizens. The very one who had enslaved them, taking them from comfortable homes to a foreign land, like going from Washington D.C. to Tehran. This king had threatened to kill them because he had a bad dream and then promoted them to serve in the administration of his government—the same government that had destroyed their homes and nation.

How could they accept these positions? Weren't they betraying their people, their nation, their families? What if they took the jobs and then carefully undermined Nebuchadnezzar's kingdom from the inside out?

Interesting thoughts, but all are wrong because they are based upon a false premise. King Nebuchadnezzar did *not* promote this band of four. God did! "...the Most High God is sovereign over all kingdoms on earth and sets over them anyone he wishes" (Dan. 5:21 NIV). They were working for God while reporting to a pagan king—a great truth that Nebuchadnezzar would also later learn.

These four men would spend their careers providing excellent work for unbelieving, ruthless kings and governments while remaining faithful to the Lord. That's **the cornerstone secret to thriving in Babylon:** No matter our role, occupation, or lack of position, we can serve the Lord faithfully by doing our job well, trusting God and His faithfulness even when our bosses make stupid decisions.

Daniel and his three friends had believed, obeyed, and witnessed a powerful Biblical truth: "The king's wrath is like the roaring of a lion, but his favor is like dew on the grass" (Prov. 19:12 NIV).

7
___

WHAT TO DO WHEN YOUR BOSS REQUIRES YOU TO BREAK GOD'S LAW?

In Chapter 6 we discussed the importance of praying for wisdom. The actual definition of wisdom is the ability to discern inner qualities and relationships. (Source: Merriam-Webster) When King Solomon was taking over his daddy's throne, the legendary King David—literal giant-killer —asked God for "wisdom and knowledge, that (he) may lead this people, for who is able to govern this great people of yours?" (2 Chron. 1:10-12 NIV). Solomon is inheriting massive wealth, power, and influence. He is second-generation wealth, nepotism in today's vernacular, taking over what the old man built, being born with a silver spoon in his mouth.

Interestingly, Solomon didn't ask God for more wealth, power, popularity, or even the ability to destroy his numerous enemies. He asked for wisdom and knowledge from God so that he would know what to do. The good news for us is that we don't have to be a king, a president, a dictator, a business owner, a manager, a writer, or a philosopher to ask God for wisdom. To quote once more from James 1:5 again, "If anyone is deficient in wisdom, he should ask God, who gives to all generously and without reprimand, and it will be given to him."

God's wisdom might be the most underutilized gift He has made available to His children, yet His wisdom is essential to being able to thrive in Babylon. Going into the workplace each day without it is like embarking on a sailing trip around the world with routes picked, supplies packed, but the boat? No Buena.

Wisdom provides the filter for all orders we receive from those in authority to flow. For example, is my boss telling me to do something against God's law or the laws of the land, or is it simply something I don't agree with or like? In most cases, when we rebel against those in authority, it's because we don't like the order, not because it's against the law, either God's or local laws.

Though this is the norm, there are times when those in charge will ask us to break God's law. Often, this temptation will come after we have received significant recognition or a promotion. When this happens, believers must rely on God's discernment and wisdom.

As we saw in the last chapter, Daniel and his companions were promoted by the grateful King Nebuchadnezzar to very high positions within his administration. God had used the four friends to provide peace to the king and save the lives of the other "wise" men in Babylon. While Nebuchadnezzar acknowledged Daniel and his friends' "Most High God," he hadn't yet submitted to him or turned away from his other gods. The king was still flamboyantly breaking God's first commandment, "You shall have no other gods before me" (Ex. 20:3 NIV).

The Bible reveals that after the amigos—Shadrach, Meshach, and Abednego—had been serving the king for a while, the king invited them to a big 'wing-ding.' That's the southern translation for 'hoe down.' Everybody who worked in a management position for the king was ordered to attend. It wasn't optional, RSVP or Regrets Only. It was an order. Similarly, we must attend meetings that are not optional, though few have the purpose or consequences of Nebuchadnezzar's wing-ding.

Ever the industrious one, Ol' Nebuchadnezzar had built a 90' x 9' golden statue of himself. It makes the fellas who order their self-portraits hung in places of honor seem darn right modest. On a side note, archaeologists have found what they believe is the foundation of this statue about six miles outside of modern Babylon.

Back to the story, this wasn't just an ego play on the king's part—it was a power play. Back in Daniel's day, rulers would seek to establish political, military, and religious authority over their people. Today, the first two are still common. The last, rare, though I have served under a few leaders who thought they could walk on water.

All of Nebuchadnezzar's leaders gathered before this giant, golden monstrosity. Some were probably struggling to keep a straight face when the king had his herald, who today would be known as the VP of Communications, read the new law of the land. The text was read, and it revealed King Neb wanted to play an old, high-stakes version of musical chairs. The herald announced when the music played, that everyone must "...bow down and pay homage to the golden statue that King Nebuchadnezzar has erected" (Dan. 4:5b NET).

There wasn't a gray area. The king was ordering all to break God's first commandment. Some audience members would have known the commandment, while others would not have known. But all would have clearly understood the next part of the herald's announcement: "Whoever does not bow down and pay homage will immediately be thrown into the midst of a furnace of blazing fire!" (Dan. 3:6 NIV).

This little corporate wing-ding just got serious. No one is smirking at that statue anymore. Bow and live, or stand and die. It just got real, a life-and-death situation. The Bible tells us that those fellas ate dirt, bowed, and paid homage when the music started. All, that is, except Shadrach, Meshach, and Abednego. They were the last Jews standing. They refused to break God's commandment.

At this point in the story, we can see one of the first examples of corporate politics. The Chaldeans, many of whom had been saved by the miracle of Daniel's dream interpretation, brought "malicious accusations against the Jews" (Dan. 3:8b NET). They poured it on thick and heavy as they went to the king, "O king, live forever! You have issued an edict, O king, that everyone must bow down and pay homage to the golden statue. But there are Jewish men whom you appointed over the administration of the province of Babylon—Shadrach, Meshach, and Abednego—and these men have not shown proper respect to you, O king. They don't serve your gods and they don't pay homage to the golden statue that you have erected" (Dan. 3:9b, 10a, 12 NIV).

Their complaints sounded playground-ish and pre-school-ish, but nothing was childish about their motives. These men knew the king's character, that he had a history of making clear edicts and enforcing them. Their complaint revealed the motivation of their bigoted hearts. Referring to the three amigos as Jews, not as an adjective but a blatant racial slur, showed that the Babylonians considered themselves better than Jews. Their motivation for tattle-tailing was clear. They resented serving under the authority of Shadrach, Meshach, and Abednego, who the king had placed over the province of Babylon.

The fact that Daniel and his friends had graciously used the miracle of the dream interpretation to ask the king to spare the lives of the Babylonian counselors was lost on these Chaldeans. They had witnessed the miracle and received mercy, yet they demanded that the king roast these men whom God had used to save their lives.

An angry king can be a dangerous thing. However, a person of low earthly standing, wholly submitted to honoring the Lord, can be used to humble and calm even the most potent earthly tyrants. After all he'd done for these three, Nebuchadnezzar was enraged. He'd spared their lives in Jerusalem, brought them safely to Babylon, housed them well, educated them, fed them the finest foods, and even put them into powerful positions. And how had they rewarded his kindness? By refusing to bow down and worship him at his big corporate wing-ding.

Please note, there is no evidence that the three amigos encouraged rebellion against the king's order. They were at the meeting as instructed, but quietly stood when the music began to play. Their hearts were not bent on rebellion against the king's authority but upon obedience to God's authority.

In his Babylonian way, the king offered Shadrach, Meshach, and Abednego mercy. After all, good help is hard to find. "Now if you're ready, when you hear the sound of the horn, flute, zither, trigon, harp, pipes, and all kinds of music, you must bow down and pay homage to the statue that I had made. If you don't pay homage to it, you will immediately be thrown into the midst of the furnace of blazing fire," Nebuchadnezzar offered (Dan. 3:15a NET). Southern translation, "Bless your little hearts. Maybe y'all didn't hear me. When ya hear the fiddle, take a knee. Don't make me come down there and whoop ya."

However, the king's following statement revealed the real battle that was going on that day, "Now, who is that god who can rescue you from my power?" (Dan. 3:15b NET). This wasn't about the king's authority over his people. The Lord had placed him on his throne (Jer. 27:6). This was about God's authority over the king.

Shadrach, Meshach, and Abednego's response was pure wisdom from God, "We do not need to give you a reply concerning this. If our God whom we are serving exists, he is able to rescue us from the furnace of blazing fire, and he will rescue us, O king, from your power as well. But if he does not, let it be known to you, O king, that we don't serve your gods, and we will not pay homage to the golden statue that you have erected" (Dan. 3:16-18 NET).

Secret to Thriving in Babylon: The ridiculous does not need to be debated by anyone. Answered? Yes. Debated? No.

There was no need to argue that God's power was more significant than the king's. God doesn't call us to be his defense lawyers, but to be his witnesses. Instead of debating God's power, they explained what they had experienced about the Lord. These three were on the proverbial witness stand and they answered with simple facts. Paraphrased, they said, "We are serving our God. He's able to rescue us from your hand. But even if he chooses not to rescue us, let the record show that we never broke God's first commandment by worshipping your statue." A simple witness is more powerful than debate.

That's a 'drop-the-mic' moment. The facts were clearly declared, and their statements reveal a powerful truth about properly-focused faith. They were fixated purely on the heart of God, desiring to enjoy a strong relationship with the Lord by obeying His first commandment. They were not focused on the hand of God; that is, what they would receive as a reward from the Lord for their obedience.

Secret to Thriving in Babylon: Be content to do what is right in the Lord's sight without concern for reward. The Lord's way is always right. Therefore, whatever He does can be trusted.

As stated earlier, never be surprised when a Babylonian behaves like a Babylonian. Nebuchadnezzar was so furious with Shadrach, Meshach, and Abednego that his face became distorted with rage. He commanded that the furnace be heated seven times hotter than usual. Then he ordered some of the strongest men of his army to bind Shadrach, Meshach, and Abednego and throw them into the blazing furnace. So they tied them up and threw them into the furnace, fully dressed in their pants, turbans, robes, and other garments. And because the king, in his anger, had demanded such a hot fire in the furnace, the flames killed the soldiers as they threw the three men in. So Shadrach, Meshach, and Abednego, securely tied, fell into the roaring flames (Dan. 3:19-23).

The king was in an uncontrollable rage. He ordered the furnace to be taken to a level to match his anger; thus, the results demonstrated the danger of wrath. The three companions were bound and tossed into the furnace, but the king's rage caused collateral damage as the intense heat killed his soldiers. He also inadvertently demonstrated the wisdom of the Bible, "Fools give full vent to their rage, but the wise bring calm in the end" (Prov. 29:11 NIV). "For human anger does not accomplish God's righteousness" (James 1:20 NET).

Secret to Thriving in Babylon: When life goes against you, rage is never the wise response.

Shadrach, Meshach, and Abednego showed no anger or fear while the fellow allegedly in control lost his mind. Telling somebody off or responding in anger to your boss may feel good for a moment, but there will undoubtedly be collateral damage. How many people do you love that depend on your paycheck? Please don't get them burned up by your overheated furnace. Instead, replace rage with a humble witness.

The king's wing-ding was officially out of his control, and everyone gathered there witnessed God's power. "King Nebuchadnezzar was startled and quickly got up. He said to his ministers, "Wasn't it three men that we tied up and threw into the fire?" They replied to the king, "For sure, O king." He answered, "But I see four men, untied and walking around in the midst of the fire! No harm has come to them! And the appearance of the fourth is like that of a god!" (Dan. 3:24-25 NET).

The one who claimed to be a god encountered the one true God. Three men humbly chose to obey the Lord's commandment, submitted to the king's wrongful judgment and trusted the Lord with the outcome. The king would now have eyes to see the one true God who is willing and able to save His people.

"Then Nebuchadnezzar approached the door of the furnace of blazing fire. He called out, "Shadrach, Meshach, and

Abednego, servants of the most high God, come out! Come here!"

"Then Shadrach, Meshach, and Abednego emerged from the fire. Once the satraps, prefects, governors, and ministers of the king had gathered around, they saw that those men were physically unharmed by the fire. The hair of their heads was not singed, nor were their trousers damaged. Not even the smell of fire was to be found on them!" (Dan. 3:26-27 NET).

The king was powerful and often harsh, yet he was also an honest skeptic. He had witnessed an incredible phenomenon, and so had everyone else present that day. He didn't deny it was a miracle; he accepted it. His following words revealed the reason why God performs miracles.

"Nebuchadnezzar exclaimed, 'Praised be the God of Shadrach, Meshach, and Abednego, who has sent forth his angel and has rescued his servants who trusted in him, ignoring the edict of the king and giving up their bodies rather than serve or pay homage to any god other than their God!' (Dan. 3:28 NET)."

And what is the reason God performs such wonders? So that others will see, believe, and be saved. Sure the one who receives the miracle benefits, but God's purpose is to reveal His mercy, power, and love to those who witness the miracle.

The king had gone from self-admiration to Godly proclamation. He stood as a witness, even though he didn't fully understand everything he had seen. Nebuchadnezzar wasn't a theologian. He simply explained loudly, for all to hear, what he had seen. He knew that their God had rescued them because they had chosen to obey the Lord's commandment rather than the king's edict.

King Nebuchadnezzar, excited by what he had witnessed, chose to worship God in his uniquely Babylonian way with a new law for the land.

"'I hereby decree that any people, nation, or language group that blasphemes the God of Shadrach, Meshach, or Abednego will be dismembered and his home reduced to rubble! For there exists no other god who can deliver in this way. Then Nebuchadnezzar promoted Shadrach, Meshach, and Abednego in the province of Babylon'" (Dan. 3:29-30 NET).

After one hot encounter with the Lord, the king had gone from public blasphemer to God's enforcer. Remember, never be surprised when a Babylonian behaves like a Babylonian. Nebuchadnezzar's new law, "I'll kill you and everything you love if you say anything bad about God," was his way of worshipping the Lord. It would take years for the king to understand everything that had happened that day. He didn't comprehend that God didn't need a new law to protect His people. Hadn't the furnace revealed that fact? Ol' Nebuchadnezzar didn't realize that God had called him to be a witness, not an enforcer.

However, the Lord used the king's enthusiasm for a good purpose. The new edict protected the Jews, allowing them religious freedom while living under Babylonian rule. The Lord didn't change Babylon's government, laws, or courts. A synagogue on every corner was not mandated. Rather, the king's order made known throughout Babylon what the Lord had established from the beginning: God is willing and able to protect those who believe in His name. Can I get an amen from an Egyptian pharaoh who famously heard the Lord declare through Moses, "Let my people go?"

Nebuchadnezzar's spiritual journey resembles many of us today who come to faith later in life. When we first believe, we are very excited and become too zealous to make others obey God's commandments. However, as we grow in our relationship with the Lord, we learn that giving away the love and mercy we have received from Him to others is more powerful than any decree. We, too, learn to be witnesses, not enforcers.

This chapter can't be brought to a close without pointing

out that the king promoted Shadrach, Meshach, and Abednego after the miracle of the furnace. As a result, they would be more powerful within the Babylonian government than ever before. Later we will discover that these promotions weren't for the purpose of transforming the political structure of Babylon, but for an eternal purpose that is still saving lives today.

Be careful not to fall for a shallow understanding of Christianity that teaches that the promotion of these three friends will also be your outcome in your career if you obey God. This is not the message the Lord is revealing in these passages. The significance of the promotions to believers today is much simpler—and more powerful.

The group's decisive actions reveal what any believer can apply today. First, they reported to work. Then, there was no complaining about being there; and lastly, the three went along with everything until their boss required them to break one of God's Ten Commandments. They didn't call attention to themselves, nor question the king's authority to make such a command. There were no press conferences, social media posts, or interviews demanding their rights. They stated their faith and acknowledged the king's earthly authority to toss them into the microwave. They were willing to trust God with whatever outcome He determined best. Instead of standing against the king, they were standing with God.

Secret to Thriving in Babylon: Focus on standing with God rather than against the wrongs of Babylon—and never miss a meeting.

In my business career, there have been many times I have been called before compelling people to provide answers to their questions. When I was younger, I viewed these opportunities as a way to promote myself. However, after I became a believer in Christ, the Lord changed my heart. I learned to ask God to give me the answers my bosses needed and to expect nothing but the honor of delivering the information. Sometimes I was financially rewarded, but most often I was not. But, I received something much better than worldly wealth or position: peace in knowing that I had stood with God as a witness to His love, peace, mercy, righteousness, wisdom, and joy—available to all who trust in Jesus Christ.

"May God's mercy, peace, and love be yours in abundance" (Jude 2 NET).

8

MY GOD-GIVEN PURPOSE?

"My job isn't fulfilling." "I'm powerless; without influence." "My bosses don't appreciate me, and they don't listen to me." "If only I could get a new job, things would be different." "What is my purpose, anyway?"

Ever heard yourself muttering words like these? These words are like chasing the wind, destined for failure. When we embrace the Creator of the heavens and earth—our real Boss— we live in the reality that, through our work, we are playing our small role in God's big plan—which doesn't condemn people, but saves all who believe. We will see miracles happen in our workplaces by being diligent, respectful, honest, and persevering in these virtues. But it takes time.

Daniel and his friends had been hard-working and conscientious in serving King Nebuchadnezzar for close to thirty years before they witnessed a miracle of faith that changed Babylon forever. Finally, the king had acknowledged the one true God, but he had not placed his faith in the Lord. Instead, King Nebuchadnezzar was still a pagan, embracing any false god he thought could benefit his kingdom's agenda, "Ah, we are meeting Baal worshippers at 2 pm. Grab the Baal statue out of the prop closet, have catering pull together a Baal buffet, serve the new Baal seltzer, and at the end of the day, we'll collect our taxes, sending them home full, drunk, and happy."

If Daniel had lost sight of who he was serving in Babylon during all those years, he likely would have plotted to undermine Nebuchadnezzar or even plot rebellion. But instead, living by faith, *Daniel had learned to obey and honor the Lord while serving a harsh boss.* As a result, he would witness one of the greatest miracles of faith in world history.

The king told the story of his journey to faith through a written proclamation written to his vast kingdom and carefully preserved in the Book of Daniel: "'I, Nebuchadnezzar,' the king wrote, 'was at home in my palace, contented and prosperous. I had a dream that made me afraid. As I was lying in bed, the images and visions that passed through my mind terrified me'" (Dan. 4:4-5 NIV). He then repeated the error he had before, "I commanded that all the wise men of Babylon be brought before me to interpret the dream for me ... the magicians, enchanters, astrologers and diviners..." (Dan. 4:6-7a NIV). He's seeking counsel from the same group that had failed to interpret his dreams almost thirty years earlier. Same advisors, same result. No answers for ol' Neb.

Secret to Thriving in Babylon: Don't be surprised or discouraged when leaders seek wisdom from idiots with titles. Keep praying and working. If you have the wisdom your boss needs and they are ready to accept it, the Lord will make a way for the message to be delivered.

After the initial failure, the king remembered Daniel, the one whose God had given the ability to interpret dreams. "I said, 'Belteshazzar (Daniel's Babylonian name), chief of the magicians, I know that the spirit of the holy gods is in you, and no mystery is too difficult for you. Here is my dream; interpret it for me'" (Dan. 4:9 NIV).

Think about it: After serving the king for about thirty years, Daniel was still referred to as "the chief of magicians." Magicians of that time were frauds, and the Lord had commanded believers not to have anything to do with them, yet Daniel showed no sign of offense. He knew the king meant it as a compliment.

Confession time: I used to hate being called Timmy. My mom liked to tell the story that when I was about six years old, I explained that I was now too old to be called Timmy. Many years later, I worked for a boss who always called me Timmy. It offended me because I thought he was trying to belittle me. While working for him, I came to faith in Christ. After this, I had the heart to understand that my very formal boss called me Timmy as a term of endearment. I learned to cherish when he called me by that name.

Secret to Thriving in Babylon: Don't take offense at what the boss calls you. Stay focused on serving them as if serving the Lord.

So, Nebuchadnezzar laid out the crazy dream that was haunting him. Daniel's reaction to the nightmare is a lesson for us all. "Belteshazzar answered, 'My lord, if only the dream applied to your enemies and its meaning to your adversaries!'" (Dan. 4:19b NIV). Daniel showed great concern for Nebuchadnezzar. He didn't wish harm or failure upon his boss.

It's safe to say that most of us will never work for anyone as powerful and difficult as King Nebuchadnezzar. So how do we react when we realize that our boss' decisions could result in their downfall? Do we rejoice? Do we plot for their ruin? Kick 'em while they're down? Position ourselves to take their position?

Secret to Thriving in Babylon: Be concerned for your boss' well-being and work to help them succeed. Pray for them, work hard, tell the truth, and make sure they know you care for them.

Daniel interpreted the dream. Now, the most powerful man in the world was about to be humbled by God Most High. Everything the king had worked for, all his wealth, position, wisdom, and power, were going to be stripped away, not by an opposing nation but by the Creator of the heavens and earth. The Lord was using Nebuchadnezzar to expose an incredible truth: "...that the Most High is sovereign over all kingdoms on earth and gives them to anyone He wishes" (Dan. 4:25b NET).

This declaration of God's sovereignty is a clear statement; there is no gray area. It is God's truth. But, do we believe it? Embrace it? Do we live in God's reality regarding the leaders of this world? If not, we'll never enjoy the peace that transcends all understanding in this chaotic world. We shouldn't wait until we get to heaven to realize how much time we have wasted worrying about someone else's job: God's.

Secret to Thriving in Babylon: Embrace God's sovereignty over all kingdoms on earth, and you will find a purpose and contentment by doing the next right thing each day.

Daniel knew and understood God's authority. He knew that God had empowered Nebuchadnezzar to conquer his beloved homeland, Judah. *Submission to God's authority allowed his faith and trust to grow in Babylon, rather than weaken.* He also was very aware of God's mercy, which was revealed in the dream: "The command to leave the stump of the tree with its roots means that your kingdom will be restored to you when you acknowledge that Heaven rules. *Therefore, Your Majesty, be pleased to accept my advice:* Renounce your sins by doing what is right, and your wickedness by being kind to the oppressed. It may be that then your prosperity will continue" (Dan. 4:26-27 NIV).

Those of us not called by God to be the boss can learn from Daniel's example. He cared for Nebuchadnezzar's well-being, revealed truth that was difficult for him to hear, and then offered personal advice on how the king might be able to avoid a disaster. He knew the king was guilty of great sin and wickedness, but would Nebuchadnezzar turn from these things and do right, or would he face God's judgment? Daniel showed what it means to live in Babylon as a man after God's own heart.

Daniel had provided the king exactly what he had asked for —a correct interpretation of his dream. He also used the opportunity to reveal God's compassion through his concern for him and even a way to avoid disaster. That day at work, thousands of years ago, Daniel had simply done the next right thing. He was not responsible for what the king would do with the truth.

So, Nebuchadnezzar heard the truth from a trusted advisor and leaped into action, turning from his wicked ruthlessness, ordering an end to the oppression of the weak and free raisin cakes, donkeys, honey, and wine for all. *Of course, he didn't!* The Bible's not a fairy tale; it's reality and God's truth. Think about it: Proud and influential leaders typically don't change their ways overnight, particularly when everything is going well. The Bible tells us, "Twelve months later, as the king was walking on the roof of the royal palace of Babylon, he said, 'Is not this the great Babylon *I have built* as the royal residence, *by my mighty power* and *for the glory of my majesty?*'" (Dan. 4:29-30 NIV).

Oops, somebody missed the memo regarding God's sovereignty.

"Even as the words were on his lips, a voice came from heaven, 'This is what is decreed for you, King Nebuchadnezzar: Your royal authority has been taken from you" (Dan. 4:31 NIV).

Secret to Thriving in Babylon: We are responsible for doing the next right thing with love and compassion. However, we are not responsible for how our leaders react to the truth. Therefore, we do our job knowing that God will do His.

The humbling of a mighty king had begun. The Lord would do it in such a creative and unique manner that, thousands of years later, it still stands as the ultimate statement regarding His sovereignty over all the kingdoms and nations of the earth: "'You (Nebuchadnezzar) will be driven away from people and will live with the wild animals; you will eat grass like the ox. Seven times will pass by for you until you acknowledge that the Most High is sovereign over all kingdoms on earth and gives them to anyone he wishes'" (Dan. 4:25 NIV).

"Immediately what had been said about Nebuchadnezzar was fulfilled. He was driven away from people and ate grass like the ox. His body was drenched with the dew of heaven until his hair grew like the feathers of an eagle and his nails like the claws of a bird" (Dan. 4:32-33 NIV).

Before you can spell Nebuchadnezzar, the Lord transformed the powerful king into 'cray-cray.' The man literally thought he was an ox. Instead of eating from the royal palace filled with fine foods, wines, and concubines, he ate grass in the royal meadow. Ancient Babylon had a zoo featuring animals from the nations that God had allowed them to conquer. Imagine the old tour guide, "Now just to the left of the *Lions of Judah* exhibit, you can see Ol' Nebuchadnezzar grazing with the royal heifers."

The king's madness continued for seven years. "'At the end of that time, I, Nebuchadnezzar, raised my eyes toward heaven, and my sanity was restored'" (Dan. 4:34 NIV). The Lord had re-established Nebuchadnezzar's authority and revealed the extreme lengths He was willing to utilize to reveal Himself to those who do not believe. It took seven years of grazing in a meadow, but this time, Ol' Neb received the Lord's message.

"'Then I praised the Most High;' the king wrote, 'I honored and glorified him who lives forever.
'His dominion is an eternal dominion;
his kingdom endures from generation to generation.
All the peoples of the earth
are regarded as nothing.
He does as he pleases
with the powers of heaven
and the peoples of the earth.
No one can hold back his hand
or say to him: "What have you done?'

"At the same time that my sanity was restored, my honor and splendor were returned to me for the glory of my kingdom.

My advisers and nobles sought me out, and I was restored to my throne and became even greater than before'" (Dan. 4:34b-36 NIV).

Daniel had brought glory to the Lord by working for a pagan king for thirty-plus years. During this time, he never plotted or rebelled against the king's authority. There is no evidence that Daniel even used passive resistance, the art of not doing your best. Daniel had done his job, and now he could see God's purpose in his work. God demonstrated His authority while He also revealed His heart. The Most High God wanted to save the king from false gods and use him to point all of Babylon to faith in the only One who can save.

"'Now I, Nebuchadnezzar, praise and exalt and glorify the King of heaven, because everything he does is right and all his ways are just. And those who walk in pride he is able to humble.'" (Dan. 4:37 NIV).

Secret to Thriving in Babylon: Always remember that your boss needs Christ more than you need a new boss.

There is no greater sacrifice than for a person to give up their life for another. The Lord is not asking most of us to sacrifice our lives for our Babylonian rulers, but He is asking us to sacrifice our pride. Remember, pride leads to our downfall. God wants us to humble ourselves and work in Babylon as if working for Him. By doing so, we are fulfilling our purpose in God's big plan. Though we may not obtain worldly wealth, power, or fame, we do receive something more valuable—daily contentment, peace, and even joy as we fulfill our God-given purpose. Maybe one day we will hear our Babylonian boss echo King Nebuchadnezzar's proclamation of faith.

"'I, King Nebuchadnezzar,
To the nations and peoples of every language, who live in all
the earth:
May you prosper greatly!
It is my pleasure to tell you about the miraculous signs and
wonders that the Most High God has performed for me.
How great are his signs,
how mighty his wonders!
His kingdom is an eternal kingdom;
his dominion endures from generation to generation'" (Dan.
4:1-3).

9

CHANGE IS A REALITY

I n his day, King Nebuchadnezzar was the most powerful man in the world. Today, his story would be the equivalent of the Chairman of China's Communist Party announcing, "I believe Jesus Christ is exactly who He said He was, the Son of God. I am now a Christian." God had used Daniel to change the course of the king's life through thirty-plus years of service within a pagan government.

After Nebuchadnezzar came to faith in the one true God, he returned to his small role in God's big plan as king. Now, he would be a king after God's own heart, ruling in righteousness rather than selfishness. The last recorded words from King Neb revealed his new heart and outlook:

"At that time my sanity returned to me. I was restored to the honor of my kingdom, and my splendor returned to me. My ministers and my nobles were seeking me out, and I was reinstated over my kingdom. I became even greater than before. Now I, Nebuchadnezzar, praise and exalt and glorify the King of heaven, for all his deeds are right and his ways are just. He is able to bring down those who live in pride" (Dan. 4:36-37 NET).

Don't miss the king's testimony. One of the most successful

and influential men in world history has been telling us for thousands of years, "I became greater than before." After he placed his faith in God, he *became more significant than before.* God does not bring us to faith to make us miserable. Faith allows us to be who God created us to be, which is greater than anything we can do on our own.

Think of Daniel's joy as he now served a believing king. Think of the generations that the king's conversion would impact. God accomplished all this through a small group of captives who served their captors as if serving God Himself. So, likewise, any believer in Christ fulfills their role in God's big plan when they do their jobs as if working for God.

But the Bible is not a fairytale. It is reality, and change is a reality. So, after years of faithful service to King Nebuchadnezzar, Daniel and his friends experienced a dramatic change. King Nebuchadnezzar died after ruling Babylon for about forty-three years. Daniel would serve under four more Babylonian kings. Each king was less talented and less wise than their predecessor. There is no evidence that any of these kings came to faith in God. Instead, they ignored Nebuchadnezzar's proclamation of faith. As God had already revealed through Daniel and others, though few realized it at the time, Babylon's power and influence were in steep decline.

With each new king, Daniel's influence within the Babylonian government decreased. Trusted advisors losing power under new leadership is still common. An employee works hard for a company, and their boss often seeks their opinion. But when a new boss takes over, bringing in their people, the once-valued views of the long-term employee are no longer desired or appreciated. Over time, the new boss diminishes the long-term employee's role as they represent the past, not the future. This is stinkin' thinkin' on behalf of the new boss and can be so discouraging to the long-time employee. But, when the employee realizes that they are working for God and not their new boss, confidence and assurance replace discouragement and frustration.

Think about it: When Jesus the Messiah, the Son of God, walked on this earth, he was the Boss of nothing even though He had created everything. He never ran a business or held public office. Christ submitted Himself to the earthly authorities of His day, knowing that many of them were foolish. After all, He knew that His Father had placed them in their positions. By submitting to their authority, He set the example for all believers. If the Son of God submitted Himself to unwise bosses, who am I to refuse to do the same?

The first three kings that Daniel served after serving Nebuchadnezzar were so below par that Daniel didn't even bother mentioning them in his book. However, the last of the four, King Belshazzar, serves as one of the best object lessons in all the Scriptures. Daniel described the events about thirty-two years after King Nebuchadnezzar's death. This means that Daniel was likely in his eighties when he arrived at a roaring royal party on a fateful night.

King Belshazzar is the classic example of a selfish, clueless leader. Babylon had been in decline for decades. The Persian Empire was coming into its own. In fact, much of the Babylonian Kingdom established during Nebuchadnezzar's reign had been conquered by the powerful Persians. At the time of Daniel's story, the city where King Belshazzar lived was surrounded and under siege by the Persian army.

Though surrounded, King Belshazzar was pridefully unconcerned. He had undoubtedly prepared the city for a long siege. A well-equipped army guarded large, impenetrable walls with a river that flowed through the city for water. Twenty years' worth of stored food supplies had the king in good spirits.

So, what does a selfish, clueless, arrogant leader do when facing a significant problem? Throw a party, of course! What better way is there to display confident leadership? Wouldn't you have liked to have been listening to the king and his advisors when they came up with this idea?

Let's pretend the conversation went something like this...

"So, Belshy, here's the situation: Those annoying Persians are at it again," declared Shmoozy.

"Persians? Shmersians. Are those the same guys that caused the cancellation of my summer vacation on the Med?" said King Belshazzar.

"You are spot-on, King," said Shmoozy. "They invaded our cities. They've been pillaged, raped, and destroyed. Hurt a lot of our people."

"I remember. They destroyed my favorite soft serve ice cream shop. I loved that place. They always gave me extra sprinkles," replied the king, "Maybe we could build one here at the palace? We could name flavors after my kids!"

"But, Belshy, what about the Persians?"

"Great idea! We could franchise it to them!"

"Sir, the Persians are *here*. They've surrounded the city with their army."

"*Here?* That's who's making all the noise at night?"

"There are hundreds of thousands of them just outside the walls."

"Oh, my. Our soft serve ice cream concept is not ready for them. We don't even have a logo. Way too early to talk franchising."

"Your Highness, the Persians have come to conquer the city."

"Do they know who I am? How dare they! It's laughable that they even think such a thing is possible. Have you seen our defenses? Our army? Our supplies? The Persians will grow weary of their futile siege long before we run out of soft serve, so I'm unconcerned about this Persian threat."

Realizing where the king's head was (he was sitting on it), Shmoozy decided to go with the flow.

"Most high king, this is a great opportunity to show leadership. The best way to show your confidence in our defenses is to throw a big party, the biggest of all time. We'll be so loud that the Persians will hear it. They'll be shivering in the cold outside the walls while we're partying loud and proud. How demoralizing for them."

"Brilliant! Wine. Women. Food. Music ... and more wine! Get all the stars here. The best musicians, too. Make it so, Belshy! And don't forget the soft serve."

It was indeed a poor bunch of leaders that thought a party during a siege was a good idea. While the rant above is fictional, what actually took place is even more outlandish.

Secret to Thriving in Babylon: Even though some leaders will make foolish, uninformed, self-centered decisions, God will use their folly for His glory.

The Bible tells us, "King Belshazzar prepared a great banquet for a thousand of his nobles, and he was drinking wine in front of them all. While under the influence of the wine, Belshazzar issued an order to bring in the gold and silver vessels—the ones that Nebuchadnezzar his father had confiscated from the temple in Jerusalem—so that the king and his nobles, together with his wives and his concubines, could drink from them. So they brought the gold and silver vessels that had been confiscated from the temple, the house of God in Jerusalem, and the king and his nobles, together with his wives and concubines, drank from them. As they drank wine, they praised the gods of gold and silver, bronze, iron, wood, and stone" (Dan. 5:1-4 NIV).

The king is mocking the Persians with his outrageous party. However, in a drunken stupor, his true heart is revealed. He abused all the golden vessels and cups used to worship the one true God in the Temple of Jerusalem. These vessels were sacred instruments, yet Belshazzar used them for an ungodly purpose, the drunken worship of false gods, and thus mocked the true God. He should have stuck to the red Solo cups.

Why does God hate idols and false gods? Because they are worthless. They may look good, but they're useless; they don't work. Idols are blind, deaf, mute, and lifeless. Those who make them and trust them will become like them—unable to see, hear, and speak the truth (Psa. 135:15-18). Idol worshippers waste what God has given them.

Secret to Thriving in Babylon: Don't make your career, job, or profession into an idol. Be working to live rather than living to work.

The Bible says, "Do not be deceived: God cannot be mocked. A man reaps what he sows" (Gal. 6:7 NIV). "Whoever remains stiff-necked after many rebukes will suddenly be destroyed—without remedy" (Prov. 29:1 NIV). God's patience is unfathomable, but even He has limits. The king has gone too far. Now we shall see that the Lord's way of dealing with degenerates is incredibly creative.

As the king is drunkenly toasting false gods with God's property, "At that very moment the fingers of a human hand appeared and wrote on the plaster of the royal palace wall, opposite the lampstand. The king was watching the back of the hand that was writing. Then all the color drained from the king's face and he became alarmed. The joints of his hips gave way, and his knees began knocking together" (Dan. 5:1-3 NET).

That's a buzz kill. The king sees the fingers of a human hand writing on the wall of his royal palace. In a few seconds, the 'hand of God' wrote a quick message and accomplished what the Persian army could not—terrifying the king into a knee-knocking, cartoonish stupor.

The king went into a complete panic. He did what people in great power usually do. He called the "experts" to come immediately to examine the writing on the wall. What could it mean? No one had any answers, so he offered a fantastic reward. He offered the number three position in his government for the person who had the correct answer. Crickets.

The party turned into a panic fest. Suddenly, it wasn't fun anymore. The king's terror and anxiety had spread throughout the banquet hall like locusts through a wheat field, consuming all. Ironically, the noise from their panic was so loud that it got the attention of the king's mama, who wasn't even attending the party. When she realized the problem, she said, "Don't be alarmed! Don't be shaken! There is a man in your kingdom who has within him a spirit of the holy gods. In the days of your father, he proved to have insight, discernment, and wisdom like that of the gods … Daniel, whom the king renamed Belteshazzar, an extraordinary spirit, knowledge, and skill to interpret dreams, explain riddles, and solve difficult problems. Now summon Daniel, and he will disclose the interpretation'" (Dan. 5:10b, 12 NET).

Even a drunk king knows you'd better listen to your mama. So, the king summoned the fella named Belteshazzar. How forgotten was Daniel by the leadership of Babylon? When he entered the party room, "The king said to Daniel, 'Are you that Daniel who is one of the captives of Judah…?'" (Dan. 5:13 NET). Daniel was so far removed from the earthly power of King Belshazzar that the king didn't even know to ask for him. After seventy-five plus years of living and working in Babylon, the one in authority over him would still refer to him as "one of the captives of Judah." Unlike Nebuchadnezzar, King Belshazzar had no relationship with Daniel. When Daniel speaks to this king, there is no relationship.

Secret to Thriving in Babylon: The world may demote, forget, exclude, or not accept you as their own, but God knows how to put you where you need to be.

Daniel identified himself, and the king pointed out the message on the wall. He offered old, forgotten Daniel the number three spot in the kingdom if he could interpret the writing. Daniel's response was classic: "Keep your gifts, and give your rewards to someone else. However, I will read the writing for the king and make known its interpretation" (Dan. 5:17 NET).

Undoubtedly, while he wasn't part of the government's ruling class, as a citizen in Babylon, Daniel would be well aware of the king's arrogant, self-centered, incompetent leadership. Yet, there is no evidence that Daniel did anything to undermine the king's authority during the forgotten years. Now the king has summoned Daniel and asked for his opinion. Under the rules of Babylon, Daniel was permitted to speak his mind. And that, he did.

He reminded Belshazzar of the great King Nebuchadnezzar, who built and ruled the Babylonian empire with an arrogant, but gifted, iron fist. He reminded Belshazzar how God had humbled ol' Neb. He was the big draw, the cash cow for the Babylonian Zoo for seven years. But, when he was humbled and subsequently placed faith in God, his kingdom was restored and became bigger and better than before.

Secret to Thriving in Babylon: Recalling God's history builds faith and confidence. Never forget what God has done. Never grow weary of telling how He has moved in your life and in the lives of others.

Nebuchadnezzar's story ended very well. King Belshazzar made his own choices about God, though. The stories of our ancestors, relatives, parents, friends, and heroes may be inspiring, but each of us must write our own story. Every individual bears a personal responsibility to enter into a relationship with God. The Lord welcomes all who call on His name. However, "Hi, God, I never believed in you, but my great, great grandaddy did" doesn't get it done. Belshazzar was about to learn that truth.

Daniel had never flattered anyone for a favor, and he was too old to start now, "Belshazzar, you have not humbled yourself, although you knew all this. Instead, you have exalted yourself against the Lord of heaven. You brought before you the vessels from his temple, and you and your nobles, together with your wives and concubines, drank wine from them. You praised the gods of silver, gold, bronze, iron, wood, and stone— gods that cannot see or hear or comprehend. But you have not glorified the God who has in his control your very breath and all your ways" (Dan. 5:22-23 NET).

It's essential to remember that the king had asked Daniel to speak. Therefore, Daniel had the freedom to be direct. He contrasted Belshazzar's actions to Nebuchadnezzar's. Additionally, Daniel was very specific regarding why the Lord was angry. The king thought he was more significant and more powerful than God. Belshazzar's arrogance of the heart had led to the stupidity of his brain, actually chasing fantasies while ignoring the truth of the living God who has control of everything the king did, even each breath he took.

Secret to Thriving in Babylon: When an authority asks for your opinion, be factual, concise, and truthful. Flattery and "I think" usually don't go over well.

Between the effects of alcohol, fear, and the Holy Spirit, the proud and arrogant king was speechless. Daniel continued, "'Therefore the palm of a hand was sent from him, and this writing was inscribed. This is the writing that was inscribed: MENE, MENE, TEQEL and *PERES*. This is the interpretation of the words: As for M*ene*—God has numbered your kingdom's days and brought it to an end. As for T*eqel*—you are weighed on the balances and found to be lacking. As for P*eres*—your kingdom is divided and given over to the Medes and Persians'" (Dan. 5:25-28 NIV).

I wonder if this is where the phrase "talk to the hand" originated? God sent the hand, and God made Belshazzar king. The length of his rule was determined and ordained by God's sovereignty. Time was now up. The king had squandered his God-given gift of authority and position. The wealthy and powerful earthly king was found to be lacking by the eternal King of kings. Therefore, God would give the kingdom to others. The party was over.

Secret to Thriving in Babylon: Our bosses don't need our curses and rebellion. They need our prayers. God still applies *"Mene, Teqel, Peres"* to all in authority. To whom much is given, much will be required.

"I urge, then, first of all, that petitions, prayers, intercession and thanksgiving be made for all people—for kings and all those in authority, that we may live peaceful and quiet lives in all godliness and holiness. This is good, and pleases God our Savior, who wants all people to be saved and to come to a knowledge of the truth" (1 Tim. 2:1-4 NET).

The king and his court, and the untold millions—possibly billions—of people who have and will hear this story, understand that God's patience has its limits. King Belshazzar angered the Creator of heaven and earth so much that a message was clearly written for all to see, believe, and be saved.

The proud king's response to the old, forgotten servant's buzz-killing message gives hope that he asked God for forgiveness before the sun came up. Instead of anger or denial, he ordered Daniel "clothed in purple, a golden collar was placed around his neck, and he was proclaimed third ruler in the kingdom" (Dan. 5:29 NET).

The scriptures reveal—and history confirms—that under the cover of darkness on that night, the Persians pulled off an engineering wonder. The Euphrates River, which flowed through the city of Babylon, was re-routed. This feat lowered the water level and allowed the Persian troops to march under the sluice gates, quickly seize the city, and assassinate King Belshazzar.

History recorded the day that the Persians took the city of Babylon, and on our modern calendar it would be October 12, 539 BC. However, history often misses that the Persians' victory that day fulfilled the prophecies that had been given to Nebuchadnezzar over forty years earlier by Daniel in the second chapter of Daniel. Even more revealing, at least 150 years earlier, the Lord, speaking through the prophet Isaiah, also stated that He would take vengeance on the mighty nation of Babylon. "Sit in silence, go in darkness, queen city of the Babylonians; no more will you be called the queen of kingdoms" (Isa. 47:5 NIV). God knows the beginning and the end. He can be trusted.

When we remember that God is in control—yesterday, today, and tomorrow—it is easier to follow Him through the chaos of this world. We can also take great joy, no matter our social position. So, the next time you look at your boss or leaders, don't curse them. Remember, God will hold them accountable for the authority He has provided them. Instead, pray for them that they will serve as faithful followers of Christ and be found worthy by God.

10

TRUSTING GOD'S SOVEREIGNTY

A s we saw in the last chapter, change is as consistent as the sunrise. Change occurs every day. Our bodies change, circumstances, families, workplaces, and societies change daily. "There is a time for everything, and a season for every activity under the heavens" (Eccles. 3:1 NIV). The trick is to not hold onto seasons that have passed. Instead, embrace each season as it comes, knowing the same God who delivered you in the past will guide you through the future. When we trust God's sovereignty and character, we can clearly see the role we are to play.

Secret to Thriving in Babylon: Trust the One who orchestrates the change.

One of the most common transitions we will encounter happens in leadership. Our bosses change continually. Whether the new boss is better or worse than the previous boss doesn't alter our responsibility to serve as if working for the one

Boss who will never let us go or change, Jesus Christ. This head and heart perspective will lead us into circumstances beyond our imaginations while giving us peace, contentment, and even joy as we navigate through often turbulent seas. When the Lord moves a bad leader on, we workers often have two reactions. A gleeful "good-bye" and an "uh-oh, what's next." Relief followed by concern.

After Belshazzar's party ended badly, Daniel found himself on the "uh-oh" side of a leadership change. This change would be as dramatic as when he was taken from his Jerusalem home to Babylonian exile about seventy-five years earlier. So, how would an old Daniel handle this dramatic shift?

Imagine that the company you work for is sold, and you are now considered to be past your prime. When a corporation changes ownership in the United States, usually all higher-salaried, upper-management people are replaced by people from the new company. The new owners make strategic alignment changes resulting in the loss of well-compensated workers' jobs. These alignment changes impact older workers most often. We all can learn lessons from Daniel. He wasn't facing job loss; he was facing life loss.

Daniel was on the wrong end of a hostile takeover. The Babylonian empire was out; the Persians were now large and in charge. A complete regime change. How would the new ruler, King Darius, treat a lifetime, high-level government official of the conquered nation?

"It pleased Darius to appoint 120 satraps to rule throughout the kingdom, with three administrators over them, one of whom was Daniel. The satraps were made accountable to them so that the king might not suffer loss. Now Daniel so distinguished himself among the administrators and the satraps by his exceptional qualities that the king planned to set him over the whole kingdom" (Dan. 6:1-3 NIV). New boss. Same God. Same Daniel.

Yes, significant changes had occurred. But what hadn't changed was the God who was in control. Daniel had lived this truth since Babylon had first enslaved him. God was his Boss. He would serve the authority he was placed under as serving God; therefore, Daniel gave his best.

Daniel, cast aside by Belshazzar, now found great favor with the Persians. This old Jewish guy had been taken into captivity twice; to both of his captors he was a foreigner and an outsider, following some crazy God. And he was now being promoted above his Persian peers.

How did Daniel accomplish this? He "distinguished himself" among his peers because of his exceptional qualities. What were those qualities? He wasn't corrupt. He treated everyone with respect and kindness, and he walked in integrity. As a result, Darius, Daniel's new boss, could trust him.

Secret: Each day, work for God. This will make you stand out.

Think about it: Can your boss trust you? Do you work hard when they're not around? Do you tell the truth? Do you take 'sick day' vacations? Do you work the system, or do you systematically work for God?

In our Babylonian world today, it's typical—and even expected—for employees to slack off and work the system. That's why many employee handbooks are thicker than the New Testament. They're trying to protect themselves against employees that work the system: The more rule-breakers, the more rules there have to be.

I've worked in Corporate America for over thirty years. In those years, I confess that I've never read an employee handbook. Instead, I've done my best to obey three simple God Rules for the workplace.

1. Tell the Truth.
2. Work Hard.
3. Treat Everyone with Respect.

I'm not perfect. At times, I've failed at keeping these rules. But when I fail, I go to my Boss, Jesus Christ, confess my mistake, and ask what to do next. Amazingly, my Boss has never considered firing me. Instead, He forgives me and reveals how I am to do the next right thing, and by obeying those three God Rules, I've never run afoul of the employee handbook's rules of conduct, either.

We've discussed at length the importance of Christians living by this verse: "Whatever you do, work at it with all your heart, as working for the Lord, not for human masters, since you know that you will receive an inheritance from the Lord as a reward. It is the Lord Christ you are serving" (Col. 3:23-24 NIV). Please realize that following Christ in the workplace does not mean that we are destined for easy times and promotions in Babylon. Instead, we must find contentment with whatever work we are given, knowing that our full reward is in heaven. Each day, doing our best for the Lord brings satisfaction and peace, not necessarily recognition or promotion.

But sometimes these are given, and sometimes they can result in a negative downside: jealousy. We could become a target, as Daniel did. His peers learned that the king was planning to promote him to the highest government position in the land. "At this, the administrators and the satraps tried to find grounds for charges against Daniel in his conduct of government affairs, but they were unable to do so. They could find no corruption in him, because he was trustworthy and neither corrupt nor negligent." (Dan. 6:4 NIV).

Neither the administrators nor Daniel's peers, the satraps, wanted him to become their new boss. They tried to undermine him. When God is your Boss and integrity is your mode of operation, it's tough for critics, rivals, and enemies to find dirt. Daniel was honest and fair. He didn't take bribes. Ironically, his peers were completely corrupt. Therefore, they needed a boss who 'worked' the system, not a fella who would honestly work *within* the system.

Corrupt, jealous people don't give up easily, though. They can be amazingly resilient and creative. Can't find dirt on a rival? Just create it, then. "Finally, these men said, 'We will never find any basis for charges against this man Daniel unless it has something to do with the law of his God.'" (Dan. 6:5 NIV).

They spotted what they perceived to be a weakness: Daniel's faith in God. "So these administrators and satraps went as a group to the king and said, 'May King Darius live forever! The royal administrators, prefects, satraps, advisers and governors have all agreed that the king should issue an edict and enforce the decree that anyone who prays to any god or human being during the next thirty days, except to you, Your Majesty, shall be thrown into the lions' den. Now, Your Majesty, issue the decree and put it in writing so that it cannot be altered —in accordance with the law of the Medes and Persians, which cannot be repealed.' So King Darius put the decree in writing" (Dan. 6:6-8 NET).

In today's terms, Daniel's enemies were trying to use religious persecution to alienate him from the boss. It's important to understand that the king respected these administrators, the senior leaders in his government. He appreciated the "live forever" loyalty they showed. For thirty days, their idea that all must pray only to him, the majestic king, was an honor and a way of solidifying his rule within this new Persian territory. In ancient times, rulers would often claim deity to consolidate power. The death penalty for disobedience would eliminate potential enemies. It would also send a clear message that obedience to the new king's decrees was not optional. Many leaders love power, so this idea filled the king's love bucket. Deal!

Daniel's boss, employer, and country had just made a mandatory, binding law on all people that went directly against God's law. "You shall have no other gods before me. You shall not make for yourself an image in the form of anything in heaven above or on the earth beneath or in the waters below. You shall not bow down to them or worship them" (Ex. 20:3-5 NIV). Daniel had been through this before and knew that God establishes all authority in heaven and earth. He had been serving in Babylon a long time. As discussed in Chapter 7, Daniel had resolved in his heart to work for the Lord and do what was right in His sight.

Of all the edicts Daniel had received over his eighty-plus years of honorable service, this might have been the easiest one to manage without a conflict with his pagan boss. He had mastered relying on God to mitigate potential conflicts with many kings. The decree did not command him to pray to King Darius or bow down to a statue as his three amigos had been instructed. It just forbade him to pray to any god for thirty days. What if he had thought, "Heck, a fast lasts forty days." Or, Daniel might have thought, "I'm old, too tired to fight Darius, risk my life, or my promotion. I can fast from God for thirty days. I'll outlast them. He'll understand."

However, this decree was more insidious than anything Daniel had faced. It would require him to *deny* God and His commandments. If he went along with it, Daniel would be walking away from the Boss he had never seen but who he believed had diligently empowered him to overcome many challenges. Maybe Daniel recalled how Shadrach, Meshach, and Abednego had handled Nebuchadnezzar's similar order many years previous. They refused to break the same commandment, and God saved them from the fiery furnace.

With his life in the balance, Daniel's decision is an example for all Christians who face this challenge in their Babylonian lives. "Now when Daniel learned that the decree had been published, he went home to his upstairs room where the windows opened toward Jerusalem. Three times a day he got down on his knees and prayed, giving thanks to his God, just as he had done before" (Dan. 6:10 NIV).

Daniel knew who he worked for, and he wouldn't undermine his sovereign Boss, God.

Once Darius published the decree, Daniel knew that there was nothing he could do to change it. An appeal to the king would be wasted breath. The score was final. Nothing could change it. For sports fans, the call was not eligible for replay review. *Daniel couldn't change the decree, but the decree wouldn't change Daniel's relationship with God.*

Daniel had formed a habit he couldn't break—private, frequent, daily prayer with his real Boss, the Lord God Almighty. He didn't pray for show, for others to hear. He sought the Lord privately, intimately. "When you pray, go into your room, close the door, and pray to your Father, who is unseen. Then your Father, who sees what is done in secret, will reward you" (Matt. 6:6 NIV).

Daniel's prayer was a sweet aroma to the Lord. It wasn't, "You won't believe what happened at work today. Strike this pagan idiot down! Nice pick for a king. This guy's worse than that drunk man-child Belshazzar! Hey, a little help down here? They are discriminating against me. Not fair, God!" Now, I am a firm believer in being honest with God regarding our feelings. He knows them anyway, and can certainly handle our temper tantrums. So it's healthy for us to pray these frustrations out to the One who can take them and make good of them. But, how did Daniel pray? He *gave thanks!*

This prayer of Daniel's reveals his faith and trust in God. He knew that God wasn't surprised by the decree. He knew that the order was powerless. No government, no authority, can stop someone from praying to God. He also trusted God to take care of the problem. Therefore, he remained thankful for the opportunity to enjoy a relationship with the Creator of heaven and earth. Nothing can separate a believer from the great I AM.

Secret to Thriving in Babylon: Frequent, private prayer. Privately giving thanks to God when our world is falling apart demonstrates that "In God We Trust". As a result, we find the peace, strength, and courage needed to do the next right thing.

Daniel's enemies must have been surprised by his non-reaction. He had not publicly nor privately protested the king's decree. There is no indication that he even criticized the law. They had baited him with religious persecution, hoping for a public reaction of defiance that would alienate him from the king. Instead, they got the same Daniel as before—trustworthy and diligent in his duties. A new, odious decree, but the same Daniel.

Daniel understood that the workplace is not a house of worship, nor a Bible study. It is a God-ordained, neutral place that all people utilize for a common purpose—provision. Familiar with the scriptures, he knew, "A person can do nothing better than to eat and drink and find satisfaction in their own toil. This too, I see, is from the hand of God, for without him, who can eat or find enjoyment? To the person who pleases him, God gives wisdom, knowledge, and happiness, but to the sinner he gives the task of gathering and storing up wealth to hand it over to the one who pleases God" (Eccles. 3:24-26a NET).

Therefore, Daniel's honest, diligent work was pleasing to the Lord. As for his enemies, God had made a promise in the very first book of the Bible that is still true today, "I will bless those who bless you, and whoever curses you I will curse …" (Gen. 12:3a NIV).

Unfortunately for Daniel's enemies, they never sought God, so they were ignorant of His ways and their peril. Unable to spark a public act of defiance, they followed him home to dig up some dirt. Sure enough, they heard him praying, in his own home, to the Lord. Picture their excitement as they ran like ecstatic children to tattle-tale to the king.

"Hey, King Darius, remember your new decree about prayer?"

"Of course. It was the first time that you guys agreed on something. I like when everybody agrees. One of the local schools is having a pray-to-the-king contest. I'm picking a winner next week," the king responded. "Cute kids. One of them calls me King Awesome."

"Thrilled to hear you're pleased. Do you remember the penalty for disobedience?"

"Yep. The cat food clause. Haven't fed the lions in a week, just in case someone does something stupid."

The king likely thought he was having a casual conversation with his trusted advisors. He unwittingly had fallen into their legal trap. Then they said to the king, "Daniel, who is one of the exiles from Judah, pays no attention to you, Your Majesty, or to the decree you put in writing. He still prays three times a day" (Dan. 6:13 NIV).

Darius' reaction to the news revealed his respect and admiration for Daniel. "When the King heard this, he was greatly distressed; he was determined to rescue Daniel and made every effort until sundown to save him" (Dan. 6:14 NIV).

The king knew that, according to his law, the power of his decree was not reversible. So he was now facing the heavy burden of leadership. Law enforcement must be equally applied to all, without bias, or lawlessness and corruption will reign. Good leaders understand this. They don't make exceptions, and they don't make decrees for others that don't apply to themselves.

It's noteworthy that the king made every effort to rescue Daniel from the lions' den but could not find a way to do so without breaking the decree. "So the King gave the order, and they brought Daniel and threw him into the lions' den. The King said to Daniel, 'May your God, whom you serve continually, rescue you!'" (Dan. 6:16 NIV).

King Darius was as trapped as Daniel. Despite his authority, power, and wealth, he was helpless. He executed the decree with great misgivings, and Daniel was cast into the lions' den. However, closer observation provides insight into Darius' character and leadership qualities. He didn't delegate the execution. He wasn't sitting in his comfortable palace awaiting confirmation that the cats had been fed. He was right there with Daniel. He openly expressed his regret and hopelessness and unwittingly took an amazing step towards faith by publicly asking God to rescue Daniel. *For likely the first time, Daniel and the king were depending upon the same God for deliverance.*

There will be times when we find ourselves thrown into the proverbial lions' den even though we are innocent of any crime against the Lord. When we find ourselves in impossible situations, we trust God while realizing He uses our problems to open others' hearts to His glory. Maybe they, too, will learn to depend upon Christ for their deliverance.

> **Secret to Thriving in Babylon:** There will be times when we are found guilty, yet we are innocent. Trust that God is using our circumstances to help others come to faith.

The reluctant king had done the right thing. He had enforced the decree without bias. "A stone was brought and placed over the mouth of the den, and the king sealed it with his own signet ring and with the rings of his nobles, so that Daniel's situation might not be changed. Then the king returned to his palace and spent the night without eating and without any entertainment being brought to him. And he could not sleep" (Dan. 6:17-18 NIV).

A stone was placed over the lions' den and sealed by earthly authority. This stone symbolized that the wicked decree had been fulfilled. A person makes their plan and rolls the dice, but God determines the outcome. (Prov. 16:33).

The anxious king returned to his palace. He had nowhere else to go. Darius couldn't go to a shrine to pray to a false god because that would break the decree. So he had to spend the night dealing with the dilemma with only his own wisdom. Overwhelmed by his thoughts, he spent a sleepless night consumed by Daniel's situation. *The Lord used the wicked decree to help the king see his helplessness.*

"At the first light of dawn, the king got up and hurried to the lions' den. When he came near the den, he called to Daniel in an anguished voice, 'Daniel, servant of the living God, has your God, whom you serve continually, been able to rescue you from the lions?'" (Dan. 6:19 NIV).

The king didn't wait for sunrise. At first light, he ran from his palace towards the lions' den. I wonder if Darius was still wearing his fuzzy slippers? Regardless of his dress, the king looked ridiculous to any onlookers as he shouted, even before getting to the lions' den, has "the living God...rescued you...?"

Think about it. The night before, they had tossed an eighty-plus-year-old man into a pit that housed man-eating lions. The fall should have killed him before the lions gave thanks for the meal they were about to receive. Onlookers must have thought the king had lost his mind. But Darius had spent a tortuous night alone with his thoughts. He was past caring what others thought. After his efforts had failed the previous day, he knew that only God could save Daniel. Darius also needed to know if Daniel's God was real.

As the exhausted, anxious, guilt-ridden king approached, he heard a familiar voice speak words that would change his life forever. "O king, live forever! My God sent his angel and closed the lions' mouths so that they have not harmed me, because I was found to be innocent before him. Nor have I done any harm to you, O king" (Dan. 6:21b-22 NET).

There was not a hint of anger or condemnation from Daniel. The king's foolish decree placed Daniel in a horrible situation, intended to result in his death. However, he greeted the king with a blessing, "live forever." Then he provided the life-changing answers that Darius needed to hear. "Yes, God delivered me. He sent his angel that shut the mouths of the lions. I'm safe because God found me innocent. By the way, King Darius, I have never done anything to harm you" (Paraphrased).

Daniel gave a warm greeting followed by simple facts regarding what he had witnessed. No complaining, no snide, "How'd you sleep last night?" Daniel spoke lovingly and respectfully to an anxious and humbled king; he simply said what God had done. That was more than enough.

A person's reaction to the truth reveals their heart. The king's response indicates that his heart was aligned with God's will. "The king was delighted and gave an order to haul Daniel up from the den. So Daniel was hauled up out of the den. He had no injury of any kind, because he had trusted in his God" (Dan. 6:23 NET).

The king wanted Daniel safe. He got what he wanted and used his authority to haul Daniel out of the lions' den. The evidence confirmed Daniel's report. He had no injuries. Daniel's God could be trusted.

The Bible reports—and history confirms—that about 750 years later, as Jesus Christ, the Son of God, after being falsely accused and sent to his death by another evil decree, spoke from the cross to those who were murdering and mocking Him. No anger, malice, or condemnation came from His lips. He spoke what they needed to hear, not what they deserved to hear. "Father, forgive them, for they do not know what they are doing" (Luke 23:34 NIV).

Three days later, God raised his only begotten Son, Jesus Christ, undamaged and very much alive, out of the lions' den of death. We call it the Resurrection. As Daniel did for the king, Christ does for all people. See, believe, and be saved. All who believe in His name will never perish but receive the gift of eternal life, saved from all of humanity's decrees, even the foolish, evil ones. Remember, bosses need Christ, too. May our trust in Christ lead to actions that help our bosses find the truth. May we all help the kings of our lives to find God.

After the happy reunion, the king decided it was time to deal with the people who had plotted to kill Daniel. "Do not be deceived: God cannot be mocked. A man reaps what he sows. Whoever sows to please their flesh, from the flesh will reap destruction; whoever sows to please the Spirit, from the Spirit will reap eternal life" (Gal. 6:7-8 NIV). Daniel's enemies had been sowing death. They were about to bring in their harvest.

Daniel's enemies had falsely accused him. Worse, they had purposely tricked the king into a decree that would use Daniel's faith in God as the source of his destruction. A person's reaction to the truth reveals their heart. These men knew Daniel's integrity and faith in Yahweh, just as the king did. However, the king's reaction brought him peace, faith, joy, and life. The reactions of the jealous administrators and satraps reactions would bring them bitterness, anger, hate, and even death. They had proven that their wicked hearts hated God and His people.

These men dared Daniel to break God's first and second commandments, making an idol of the king and worshipping him instead of God. They thought that killing Daniel or turning him against God was a win-win plan. However, they should have read the second commandment a little closer.

"You shall not make for yourself an image in the form of anything in heaven above or on the earth beneath or in the waters below. You shall not bow down to them or worship them; for I, the Lord your God, am a jealous God, *punishing the children for the sin of the parents to the third and fourth generation of those who hate me, but showing love to a thousand generations of those who love me and keep my commandments*" (Ex. 20:4-6 NIV).

Their actions had proven that they were God-haters, bringing destruction upon themselves and their families. "The king gave another order, and those men who had maliciously accused Daniel were brought and thrown into the lions' den— they, their children, and their wives. They did not even reach the bottom of the den before the lions overpowered them and crushed all their bones" (Dan. 6:24 NET).

Before proceeding, let's address the elephant in the room. "How can God allow those innocent children to be killed?" First, your heart for children is righteous in God's sight. However, *God didn't create this mess, but He did clean it up.* Second, God had given Daniel to those wicked-hearted leaders as a witness, just as he had for Darius. Unlike Darius, however, they used God's truth to plot evil against the witness.

Next, what do you think these leaders were teaching their children (ex. The Hitler Youth)? *The Lord saved those children from being instructed in the ways of evil and welcomed them into His heavenly kingdom.* Jesus said, "Let the little children come to me, and do not hinder them, for the kingdom of heaven belongs to such as these" (Matt. 19:14 NIV). Jesus said to his disciples: "Things that cause people to stumble are bound to come, but woe to anyone through whom they come. It would be better for them to be thrown into the sea with a millstone tied around their neck than to cause one of these little ones to stumble. So watch yourselves" (Luke 17:1-3 NIV).

Rest assured, those children are playing in God's heaven today with one of my daughters. Unfortunately, however, their parents had inherited the harvest of their seeds of hatred.

Let's get back to the story. The king's actions reveal an incredible truth about a Christian's walk through Babylon. When we remain faithful to God, He will often use Babylon to fight Babylonian attacks. Daniel remained focused on following God while working hard for the authority over him. *He was steadfast in his faith and agnostic towards employers.* King Darius used Persian laws and power to punish those who plotted evil against God's innocent witness.

Secret to Thriving in Babylon: Humbly trust and obey your real Boss, Jesus Christ. He'll clean up the mess.

God used Daniel's humble act of faith to perform a miracle. Like all miracles, the recipient benefits from it, but God's purpose is for others to see, believe, and be saved. That is precisely what happened. Darius saw and believed.

"Then King Darius wrote to all the peoples, nations, and language groups who were living in all the land: 'Peace and prosperity. I have issued an edict that throughout all the dominion of my kingdom people are to revere and fear the God of Daniel.

'For he is the living God;
he endures forever.
His kingdom will not be destroyed;
his authority is forever.
He rescues and delivers
and performs signs and wonders
in the heavens and on the earth.
He has rescued Daniel from the power of the lions!'
So this Daniel prospered during the reign of Darius and the
reign of Cyrus the Persian."
— Dan. 6:25-28 NET

The king believed in the one true God. His heart was changed; he was a new creation, a new king.

A new king issued a new mandate. He sent this proclamation to all the peoples living in different cultures, speaking other languages, in all the nations throughout his dominion. He wanted them to enjoy peace and prosperity, and he was telling them how to find those things.

In other words, "Don't worship me. Forget the idols. These are worthless, expensive frauds that steal your peace and prosperity by wasting your time, talent, and money."

Darius implored all people to revere and fear the one true God, the one Daniel worshipped. To revere someone is to show deep respect or admiration to them.

"The fear of the Lord is the beginning of wisdom, and knowledge of the Holy One is understanding" (Prov. 9:10 NIV). "To fear the Lord is to hate evil; (The Lord) hates pride and arrogance, evil behavior and perverse speech" (Prov. 8:13 NIV).

This life-changing truth is applicable in any culture, in any nation, under any form of government, in any place. This truth never changes because God never changes. Yet, this never-changing truth changes one heart at a time and impacts generations forever.

Daniel knew that nothing could destroy God's Kingdom, and nothing could ever undermine His authority. But most importantly, His nature is to rescue and deliver, and He often uses supernatural acts to do so. Remember, those lions were hungry, Daniel was their meal-ticket, and their den inhospitable. These conditions differed significantly from the palace. But on that fateful morning, a healthy and peaceful Daniel emerged from the lions' den greeted by a weary king who had just arrived from his palace. *That's a great contrast between the results of God's power of deliverance versus the world's idols of wealth, power, and esteem.*

So Daniel continued to serve King Darius and his successor, King Cyrus. God would continue to prosper him under pagan governments. Daniel knew for Whom he worked. Daniel's humble act of obedience, faithfully praying to the one true God, had saved his life and revealed the truth of God's forever Kingdom and authority. The 'Daniel and the Lions' Den' story is still inspiring generations over 2,000 years later. We shouldn't be surprised, as the commandment Daniel honored came with a promise: "But showing love to a thousand generations of those who love me and keep my commandments" (Ex. 20:6 NIV).

Secret to Thriving in Babylon: Never underestimate what the Lord will accomplish through a humble and contrite heart.

11

A BOSS TO WORK FOR

Over the course of his lifetime, Daniel served seven Babylonian and Persian kings. He was never allowed to work in vocational ministry or for a Christian-owned business. Daniel didn't change the culture in which he lived. He worked and spent his entire adulthood living in a culture that did not worship the Lord. Furthermore, God never placed him on the king's throne, and He didn't make Daniel a "culture warrior." Daniel never owned anything. He never had a family, and Daniel was never accepted as 'one of us.' The culture hated him because of his race and his faith.

Indeed, by the world's measure, Daniel wasn't a success. Yet, by God's standard, Daniel was a giant.

God's amazing, eternal purposes were achieved through this humble, diligent man of integrity. Hearts have been changed for generations through his faith and trust in the character, love, and authority of the Lord, the Creator of heaven and earth, whose abounding grace and sovereignty are more powerful than any culture, government, or nation in this world.

While on Babylon's payroll, the Lord gave Daniel numerous prophecies which would validate the accuracy of the scriptures and encourage believers during God's 400 years of silence before the birth of Christ. Daniel even saw the promised Messiah, Jesus, in a vision (Dan. 7:13-14). And, while the Babylonian and Persian governments provided Daniel, Shadrach, Meshach, Abednego, and many other faithful followers of the Lord, a means of provision, these empires destroyed Judah and robbed the Lord's Temple. The Babylonians destroyed everything that had to do with the "God of the Jews" except things with a perceived monetary value. However, the exiled remnant was appointed by God to "Build houses and settle down; plant gardens and eat what they produce ..." while living in Babylon.

Yes, there is no evidence that Daniel and his three amigos ever returned to Judah or the Promised Land. As a result, they never got to spend their retirement in a Jerusalem villa on the golf course with a panoramic view of the Jordan River and Mount Zion in the background. Instead, they spent their lives living in exile, likely as eunuchs, serving pagan kings who, for the most part, would never seek the Lord. Yet, Daniel's humble witness resulted in two powerful kings choosing life-changing faith in the Lord. And in addition, he and his friends' persistent and faithful service to God has blessed untold generations for centuries.

This strong remnant honored the Lord by submitting to the earthly authority He placed over them. In return, God empowered them to thrive in a pagan culture while not turning away from their faith. But of course, they could not rely on the Holy Land's religious traditions, ceremonies, and culture to worship. Still, they learned that they could have something much better —a strong relationship with the Lord available through prayer, the scriptures, and hearts set on obedience to God.

Every time we read the Hebrew scriptures, the Old Testament, their lives are honored. While these four men and others were in exile, their positions and spare time were used to carefully transcribe the ancient scrolls—the books of Moses, Job, the Psalms, Proverbs, Isaiah, etc. Their efforts preserved God's Word for generations. That's right. God used Babylon to fund the work of protecting His scriptures!

Daniel was also a bi-vocational prophet. His prophetic writings correctly predicted the rise and fall of empires and have been used to encourage people of faith for generations and still do today.

We all live in Babylon. This is not a sin; it is a reality. May we never forget who we are serving, the Lord Jesus Christ, wherever God chooses to place us. Submitting to authority that is not directing us to break God's commandments is an act of worship. May we all do our work as if working for the Lord. When we do, we can never underestimate how God will use our humble acts to bless generations.

The Final Secret to Thriving in Babylon: There is no place on earth where someone who loves the Lord can't serve His good purpose. Through the Messiah, Jesus Christ, anyone can find the peace, wisdom, love, and joy needed to make the right decisions each day, no matter where they live or work.

As Christians, the Lord Jesus Christ is our Boss; everyone else is middle management. When we live this truth, we can serve our middle managers honorably. We also can embrace one of the great blessings Christ offers. "Come to me, all you who are weary and burdened, and I will give you rest. Take my yoke upon you and learn from me, for I am gentle and humble in heart, and you will find rest for your souls. For my yoke is easy and my burden is light" (Matt. 11:28-30 NIV)

Now that's a Boss I want to work for. How about you?

12

THE CONCLUSION OF THE MATTER

As I close this book, I'm reminded of God's sense of humor. I constantly face numerous issues in the workforce that are specifically addressed in this book. Will I practice what I preach?

The CEO of a company I worked for came to visit our facility. Although a man I did not know personally, we shared many common experiences. It was brought to my attention that the CEO was not pleased that I did not agree with one of the policies he had mandated for all business units. I obeyed his mandate precisely, never encouraged disobedience, and only revealed my opinion privately when asked by my boss. I had practiced my preaching.

Being on the endangered list of a powerful CEO in tough economic times can quickly result in transitioning to a new list —the extinction list. However, the day before the CEO arrived, the Lord finished a miraculous work. In my area of responsibility, all the goals assigned by the CEO were completed over twelve months ahead of the due date. This had never been accomplished in the company's history. Therefore, I knew I was back from the endangered list, saved from extinction for at least twelve months.

As the CEO spoke to our business unit, even a casual observer could see the contrast between us. He had authority over thousands, and I had authority over few. He had achieved great wealth, position, and recognition. I had made enough to live. So he won the battle of comparisons. He was even almost two feet taller than me.

But what many of my coworkers saw was something very different. He was a man who literally commanded an audience (attendance was not optional). However, they were drawn to the one who stood beside them, who did not lord authority over them but chose to find ways to serve them. The CEO spoke passionately on three issues that meant nothing to those gathered. The audience politely smiled, nodding in agreement as he spoke, but he was blind to the thoughts behind their smiles. The more he said, the more they realized how ill-informed he was. So, while they wisely attended, smiled, and even applauded on cue, their appreciation increased for the one who had daily been in the trenches with them.

After the CEO concluded his remarks and the audience was dismissed, one of the local employees showed up in my office. She was astonished by how disconnected the CEO was from the reality of how his policies created hardships for her. She then cried as she thanked me for being a source of encouragement and guidance each day. I don't share this story to promote myself in anyway. Instead, please see it as a source of encouragement for continuing to serve others by doing the next right thing in God's eyes.

At the end of his visit, the CEO left with his title, power, and prestige. I was left with none of the three. But I had something he did not: peace, joy, and a God-powered mission to help others at my workplace. I am truly blessed.

However, the CEO left with something else—my prayers.

May the Lord bless this CEO with love, joy, peace, and wisdom. He carries a heavy burden. I hope that he will ask Christ to take the load. May this CEO be Nebuchadnezzar, passing all he receives from the Lord to everyone he loves, meets, directs, or manages.

For your convenience, I've listed the Secrets to Thriving in Babylon from each chapter. I believe they will help you as they have helped me.

May the good Lord bless you and everyone you love.

REFLECTIONS

1

LIVE IN REALITY

Christians are a minority in a fallen world. But God always protects a remnant which only a few hold powerful positions. Most of God's remnant are like you and me—people living among and working for those who do not believe.

How does the reality that God's people are a minority living in an ungodly world change your daily expectations?

Is your faith dependent upon your culture?

How can living by faith in your current circumstances help you immediately?

2

YOU ARE A GOOD FIG

The circumstances of our birth and status in the world are not an indication of God's love and favor for His children. The good figs represented the faithful remnant exiled to Babylon, and the bad figs were the unfaithful fakers left in the Holy Land. God called the good figs to live peacefully among the Babylonians.

Living and serving in Babylon is not a punishment from God; it's an opportunity. Think about it: sending Jesus from heaven to earth was not a punishment. He came to offer freedom and salvation for all in a world dominated by Babylonian cultures. Today, we have the opportunity to help our family, friends, neighbors, and enemies in Babylon find the freedom and salvation that only Jesus Christ can provide.

How could viewing yourself as a 'good fig' change your perspective of your workplace?

Ambassadors represent their nation by living in a foreign land. Their purpose is to build a healthy, peaceful relationship for their country. The Bible calls Christians Christ's ambassadors.

How would accepting your role as Christ's ambassador change the dynamics of your relationships at work?

3

CHASING THE WIND

The workplace is a neutral zone established by God to provision people. Christians are to work as unto the Lord, not for humankind. Businesses in this world represent lifeboats, providing safety and shelter for employees.

Like Daniel, may our faith and obedience to the Lord and the earthly authority He has placed us under not be undermined by Babylon's opinions or ideas. Instead, may we enjoy the provision of Babylon, take no offense at their errors, forgive their mistakes as Christ forgives ours, and build the relationships necessary for someone to trust climbing into the lifeboat Christ has provided. We can avoid living in the frustration of chasing the wind if we do these. Instead, we can find fulfillment as we float in our God-ordained Babylonian lifeboats filled with family, friends, and former enemies. Once inside the boat, we can raise the sail to catch the wind of God's peace and provision as we ride through a chaotic world.

How can you fill your lifeboat with people perishing in a sinking world?

Daniel was able to work for ruthless Nebuchadnezzar

because he remembered who he worked for: God. How can Daniel's approach change your actions toward your boss?

4

WHAT IF YOUR EMPLOYER OFFENDS YOU?

The spirit of offense can infect people, causing them to become skewed in their beliefs and miss opportunities. Daniel revealed practical and positive ways to deal with the spirit of offense.

Seeking the Lord's solution was his primary focus. We can follow Daniel's example who was determined to obey God and not participate in Babylon's pagan dining (Dan. 1:7). There was a proper way to go about this though.

Secret to Thriving in Babylon: Private meetings with the offender—requesting, not demanding—changes can be highly effective.

How has your boss offended you? Have you privately requested changes?

5

HOW TO GET PROMOTED IN BABYLON

Daniel and his friends graduated at the top of their Babylonian class. This required them to learn many untrue things or things that went against the Lord's teachings. Yet, their faith in the Lord remained strong. They learned four secrets that can be applied today:

1. Where we are educated should not negatively impact our faith.
2. Education is the currency of Babylon.
3. Strive to become the most educated person at your workplace in whatever job you occupy.
4. Education is a cornerstone to successfully thriving in Babylon.

How can you continue to educate yourself on the best practices of your current job? What could you do to improve those best practices?

6

WHAT IF YOUR BOSS MAKES A
STUPID DECISION?

W hether they are Christians or not, leaders can make terrible decisions that cause great suffering. The authorities of this world are fallible, but that doesn't change a Christian's call to submit to the power the Lord has placed over us. God's peace comes to Christians in the workplace when we quit expecting our bosses to be perfect.

Instead, we are to seek God's wisdom to help our bosses overcome their errors

Secret: Realize that the authorities we serve can be anxious over issues we can't see.

Secret: Bring God's perspective to every problem.

At work, are you being asked to do something wrong in God's sight, or is the task just difficult to accomplish?

Secret: Know how to pray when in a tight spot.

How could consistent prayer for God's wisdom at work help you do your job?

Secret: Ask for wisdom, then receive, believe, and act on the wisdom.

When you pray, do you give the Lord your options? How

might asking God what to do without providing options change your prayer life and faith?

Secret: Remember God's wisdom is offered to all people, never to be used by anyone for self-promotion.

How can you share God's wisdom in a way that helps others do their jobs better?

Secret: Never underestimate the power of God's wisdom when received by an honest skeptic.

The **Cornerstone Secret to Thriving in Babylon:** No matter our role, occupation, or lack of position, we can serve the Lord faithfully by doing our job well as we trust God and His faithfulness.

7

WHAT TO DO WHEN YOUR BOSS REQUIRES YOU TO BREAK GOD'S LAW?

We should never be surprised that the world is filled with many legal and acceptable practices that go against God's Law. However, these conflicts create excellent opportunities to serve as an ambassador for Christ in our workplace.

How do you react to this common conflict?

Secret: Don't expect everyone to react appropriately to the Lord's miracles and mercy.

Secret: When asked to do something against God's commandments, focus on obedience to God rather than undermining earthly authority.

Secret: The ridiculous does not need to be debated by anyone.

Secret: Be content to do what is right in the Lord's sight without concern for reward. The Lord's way is always right. Therefore, whatever He does can be trusted.

Secret: When life goes against you, rage is never the wise response.

Secret: Focus on standing with God rather than against the wrongs of Babylon.

Reflections

Who can you apply these secrets to your current conflicts?

8

MY GOD-GIVEN PURPOSE?

Complaining about your job is like chasing the wind. Daniel never complained. He was diligent in doing his work with excellence while patiently waiting for God to do the same with the hearts of those in his workplace. We will see miracles happen in our workplaces by being diligent, respectful, honest, and persevering in godly virtues. But it takes time.

Secret: Don't be surprised or discouraged when leaders seek wisdom from idiots with titles. Keep praying and working. If you have the wisdom your boss needs and they are ready to accept it, the Lord will make a way for the message to be delivered.

Secret: Don't take offense at what the boss calls you. Remain focused on serving them as if serving the Lord.

Secret: Be concerned for your boss' well-being and work to help them succeed. Pray for them, work hard, tell the truth, and make sure they know you care for them.

Secret: Embrace God's sovereignty over all kingdoms on earth, and you will find a purpose and contentment by doing the next right thing each day.

Secret: We are responsible for loving and compassionately doing the next right thing. However, we are not responsible for how our leaders react to the truth. Therefore, we do our job knowing that God will do His.

Secret: Always remember, your boss needs Christ more than you need a new boss.

How can applying these secrets change your mind towards those you resent at work?

9

CHANGE IS A REALITY

Accepting that change is persistent and consistent allows a Christian to focus on navigating change rather than fighting it.

Secret: Even though some leaders will make foolish, uninformed, self-centered decisions, God will use their folly for His glory.

Secret: Don't make your career, job, or profession into an idol. Be sure to work to live rather than live to work.

Secret: The world may demote, forget, exclude, or not accept you as their own, but God knows how to put you where you need to be.

Secret: Recalling God's history builds faith and confidence. Never forget what God has done. Never grow weary of telling how He has moved in your life and others.

Secret: When an authority asks for your opinion, be factual, concise, and truthful. Flattery and "I think" usually don't go over well.

Secret: Our bosses don't need our curses and rebellion. They need our prayers. God still applies 'Mene, Teqel, Peres' to all in authority. To whom much is given, much will be required.

Which one of the "secrets" in this chapter can you apply tomorrow at work?

10

TRUSTING GOD'S SOVEREIGNTY

Change is as consistent as the sunrise. Change occurs every day. Our bodies change, circumstances, families, workplaces, and societies change daily. "There is a time for everything, and a season for every activity under the heavens" (Eccles. 3:1 NIV). The trick is to not hold onto seasons that have passed. Instead, embrace each season as it comes, knowing the same God who delivered you in the past will guide you through the future. When we trust God's sovereignty and character, we can clearly see the role we are to play.

Secret: Trust the One who orchestrates the change.

Daniel "distinguished himself" among his peers because of his exceptional qualities. What were those qualities? He wasn't corrupt. He treated everyone with respect and kindness, and he walked in integrity. As a result, Darius, Daniel's new boss, could trust him.

Secret: Each day, work for God. This will make you stand out.

Secret: Frequent, private prayer. Privately giving thanks to God when our world is falling apart demonstrates that "In God

We Trust." As a result, we find the peace, strength, and courage needed to do the next right thing.

Secret: There will be times when we are found guilty, yet we are innocent. Trust that God is using your circumstances to help others come to faith.

Secret: Humbly trust and obey your real Boss, Jesus Christ. He'll clean up the mess.

Secret: Never underestimate what the Lord will accomplish through a humble and contrite heart.

How can embracing God's sovereignty bring peace to you now?

11

A BOSS TO WORK FOR

Over the course of his lifetime, Daniel served seven Babylonian and Persian kings. He was never allowed to work in vocational ministry or for a Christian-owned business. Daniel didn't change the culture in which he lived. He worked and spent his entire adulthood living in a culture that did not worship the Lord. Furthermore, God never placed him on the king's throne, and He didn't make Daniel a "culture warrior." Daniel never owned anything. He never had a family, and Daniel was never accepted as 'one of us.' The culture hated him because of his race and his faith.

Indeed, by the world's measure, Daniel wasn't a success. Yet, by God's standard, Daniel was a giant.

God's amazing, eternal purposes were achieved through this humble, diligent man of integrity. Hearts have been changed for generations through his faith and trust in the character, love, and authority of the Lord, the Creator of heaven and earth, whose abounding grace and sovereignty are more powerful than any culture, government, or nation in this world.

The Last Secret to Thriving in Babylon: There is no place on earth where someone who loves the Lord can't serve His good purpose.

We all live in Babylon. This is not a sin; it is a reality. May we never forget who we are serving, the Lord Jesus Christ, wherever God chooses to place us. As Christians, Christ is our Boss; everyone else is middle management. When we live this truth, we can serve honorably.

"Whatever you do, work at it with all your heart, as working for the Lord, not for human masters, since you know that you will receive an inheritance from the Lord as a reward. It is the Lord Christ you are serving" (Col. 3:23-24 NIV).

12

THE CONCLUSION OF THE MATTER

Serving others by doing the next right thing in God's eyes makes us a source of encouragement and guidance for those in our workplaces each day. We can count on being blessed with peace and joy as we serve in our God-powered missions.

How have you been used to encourage or guide others at your workplace?

Do you feel God's peace knowing you have served Him by doing the right thing?

ABOUT THE AUTHOR

Tim Paskert was born in Tampa, Florida. He met his wife, Chandra, in college at Western Carolina University. They were married in 1987 and reside in Florida. Tim and Chandra have three grown children and one who lives in heaven.

Tim shares that late one evening in August of 1996, his life changed forever when, for the first time, he realized that God is real and can be trusted. Since that night, Tim's approach to life has changed. Living by the motto: "Life's too short, and so am I," he learned to treat each day as a new adventure with God, to view his family as blessings, his routine job as a gift from God, and to do his best each day to live as Jesus taught. This simple approach has allowed Tim to walk through doors of opportunity, either disasters or the usual routines of life, with joy and peace that surpasses understanding.

God has enabled Tim to serve as a Vice President and Director in some of the largest media companies in the United States, participate in medical mission trips to remote parts of the world, author two books, *The Relationship* and *Secrets To Thriving In Babylon*, as well as numerous motivational works.

Tim also wrote and produced The Glass Window movie that has been distributed worldwide, was ordained as a reverend, and had the great honor and blessing of founding and teaching the Cigar City Bible Study. In addition, he and his wife are co-founders of Mark829, a non-profit existing to help others discover the answer to the most important question in anyone's life, "Who is Jesus?"

Tim's practical, often humorous observations help readers discover the joy of following Christ through a chaotic world.

ACKNOWLEDGMENTS

God's hand has continually guided me in many miraculous ways. I am forever grateful to Him and for those He strategically placed along my path.

I will begin by acknowledging and thanking my parents, Sue and George Paskert, who taught me right from wrong and the importance of treating each and every person as I want to be treated.

A special thank you to my wife, who is the greatest blessing I have received from the Lord. Her unconditional love, secret prayers, encouragement, kindness, and wisdom makes me want to be a better man each day, one worthy of such a beautiful blessing from the Lord.

For Randy Ashcraft, my first pastor who was patient with my constant questions, the priests at Jesuit High School who continued to love me even though I was a constant "thorn" in their flesh, and for Jasper Rogers, who to this day is the most genuine Christian I have ever met.

For the Mark829 Board members: John Oliva, Mondy Flores, David Brewer, Mike Terrana, Kevin McGuinness, and Danny Someillan. You have kept me accountable, encouraged me, and constantly prayed for me, our family and the ministry. To my numerous business mentors: Joe Bourdow, David Whitaker, Mark Higgins, Paul Gordon and most of all Bill Spell. It has been an honor and privilege to serve with you in each of our different Babylons.

For the faculty and staff at Western Carolina University. My experiences there were life-changing. I was fortunate to sit under the teaching of some of the greatest business minds of our time. My professors' integrity and godly examples made a lasting impact, and one of our children has had a similarly positive experience at WCU.

For my in-laws, John and Jimmie McCorkle. Thank you for being role models, for loving me as one of your own, and for raising my wife to know the Lord Jesus.

I'd also like to thank Eli Gonzalez, for helping me edit and finalize this book.

This list is by no means exhaustive. There have been so many throughout my life that the Lord has used in small and big ways to guide me along His path. Thank you to Him and to each of you!

May all be done for the glory of Jesus Christ, the Messiah.

Made in the USA
Coppell, TX
20 July 2023

19418670R00075